# CONTENTS

# ABOUT THIS BOOK

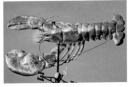

**Above:** skyline view and Charles River; statue of Paul Revere in the North End; Christian Science Plaza at night; baseball at Fenway Park, home of the Red Sox; lobster weathervane at the Waterfront.

This *Step by Step Guide* has been produced by the editors of Insight Guides, whose books have set the standard for visual travel guides since 1970. With top-quality photography and authoritative recommendations, this guidebook brings you the very best of Boston in a series of 16 tailor-made tours.

## WALKS AND TOURS

The tours in the book provide something to suit all budgets, tastes, and trip lengths. As well as covering Boston's many classic attractions, the routes track lesser-known sights and up-and-coming areas; there are also excursions for those who want to extend their visit outside the city.

The tours embrace a range of interests, so whether you are a history buff, an art-lover, a gourmet, a shopaholic, or have kids to entertain, you will find an option to suit.

We recommend that you read the whole of a tour before setting out. This should help you to familiarize yourself with the route and enable you to plan where to stop for refreshments –

options for this are shown in the 'Food and Drink' boxes, recognizable by the knife and fork sign, on most pages.

For our pick of the walks by theme, consult Recommended Tours For… *(see pp.6–7)*.

## OVERVIEW

The tours are set in context by this introductory section, giving an overview of the city to set the scene, plus background information on food and drink, shopping, sports and entertainment. A succinct history timeline highlights the key events that have shaped Boston over the centuries.

## DIRECTORY

Also supporting the tours is a Directory chapter, comprising a user-friendly, clearly organized A–Z of practical information, our pick of where to stay while you are in the city, select restaurant listings (complementing the more low-key cafés and restaurants that feature within the tours themselves), and recommended nightlife venues.

## The Author

During his career as a journalist and photographer, award-winning travel writer Simon Richmond has lived in several cities, including London, Tokyo, Sydney and Boston. He has authored and contributed to over 30 different travel guidebooks from Cape Town to the Trans-Siberian Railway, as well as restaurant and activity guides; he has worked for Insight Guides on their Step by Step Tokyo and Step by Step New England, as well as their City Guide Tokyo. Compact, historic, but also modern, Boston is, in Simon's view, one of the best cities in the world for discovering on foot.

This book builds on previous work by travel writer Marcus Brooke, who used to teach at Harvard and MIT.

## Margin Tips
Shopping tips, historical facts, handy hints and information on activities help visitors make the most of their time in Boston.

## Feature Boxes
Notable topics are highlighted in these special boxes.

## Key Facts Box
This box gives details of the distance covered on the tour, plus an estimate of how long it should take. It also states where the route starts and finishes, and gives key travel information such as which days are best to do the route or handy transport tips.

## Route Map
Detailed cartography shows the tour clearly plotted with numbered dots. For more detailed mapping, see the pull-out map slotted inside the back cover.

## Food and Drink
Recommendations of where to stop for refreshment are given in these boxes. The numbers prior to each restaurant/café name link to references in the main text. On city maps, restaurants are plotted.

The $ signs at the end of each entry reflect the approximate cost of a three-course dinner for one, excluding beverages, tax, and tip. These should be seen as a guide only. Price ranges, also quoted on the inside back flap for easy reference, are as follows:

| | |
|---|---|
| $$$$ | $60 and above |
| $$$ | $40–60 |
| $$ | $20–40 |
| $ | $20 and below |

## Footers
Those on the left-hand page give the tour name plus, where relevant, a map reference; those on the right-hand page show the main attraction on the double page.

## ESCAPING THE CROWDS

Head to the Charles River (walk 4) or to the Back Bay Fens (walk 7) for green spaces. Alternatively, the tranquil residential streets of Beacon Hill (walk 5) are generally crowd-free. For the ultimate escape, take a ferry to one of the Harbor Islands (tour 11).

# RECOMMENDED TOURS FOR...

### CHILDREN

The Aquarium and the Children's Museum (walk 10) will be hits with the little ones, as will the Museum of Science (walk 4). The USS *Constitution* in Charlestown (walk 2) and the Plimoth Plantation in Plymouth (tour 15) are both educational and fun.

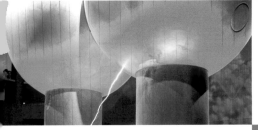

### SCIENCE & TECHNOLOGY

The Museum of Science and the MIT Museum and campus (walk 4) have outstanding boffin appeal, as do Harvard's Peabody Museum and Museum of Natural History (walk 3).

### WATERSIDE VIEWS

You are seldom far from water in Boston, be it the Charles River (walk 4) or Boston Harbor (walks 2 and 10). To get out on the water, take a ferry to the Harbor Islands (tour 11) or Provincetown, Cape Cod (tour 16).

### REVOLUTIONARY BOSTON

Follow the Freedom Trail of revolutionary sites through Boston's Downtown (walk 1), North End and Charlestown (walk 2), then head out of town to follow the 'Battle Road' between Lexington and Concord (tour 14).

## ART ENTHUSIASTS

If you love art, don't miss the Museum of Fine Arts and Isabella Stewart Gardner Museum (walk 8), or the Institute of Contemporary Art (walk 10). Salem's Peabody Essex Museum (tour 12), Cape Ann's art colonies (tour 13), and Provincetown's galleries (tour 16) are also worthwhile.

## ARCHITECTURE

Beacon Hill (walk 5), Back Bay (walk 6), and the South End (walk 9) are all packed with grand Bostonian architecture from the 17th through early 20th centuries. MIT's Stata Center (walk 4) and the Institute of Contemporary Art at Fort Point (walk 10) are fantastic 21st-century additions to the city.

## FOOD AND WINE

Dine out in either the North End (walk 2) or South End (walk 9), and your stomach will be very happy. Harvard Square (walk 3) is also a fine place to chow down, as is Newbury Street in Back Bay (walk 6).

## SHOPPERS

Check out Charles Street's antiques shops (walk 5), Newbury Street's boutiques (walk 6), Harvard's bookstores (walk 3), and the South End's quirky independent stores (walk 9).

## PARKS AND GARDENS

Boston's Emerald Necklace of parks and gardens extends from the Common (walk 1) through the Public Garden (walk 5) and Commonwealth Avenue's central boulevard (walk 6) to the Back Bay Fens (walk 7). The Charles River Esplanade (walk 4) is also a strolling pleasure.

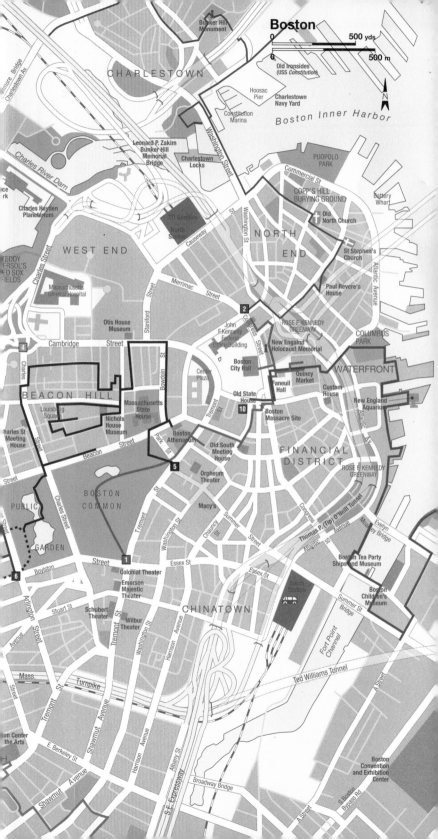

# INSIGHT GUIDES
# BOSTON
## Step by Step

**APA PUBLICATIONS** L

Part of the Langenscheidt Publishing Group

# OVERVIEW

An overview of Boston's geography, character, and culture, plus illuminating background information on food and drink, shopping, sports, entertainment, and history.

# INTRODUCTION

*Both traditional and modern, Boston is considered the most 'European' of American cities – hardly surprising given its British colonial roots. But this is also the birthplace of the country's independence, and home to some of its most illustrious Ivy League institutions.*

Boston is small (population 617,000) and compact (48.5 sq. miles/125 sq. km), making it an ideal city for discovering on foot. It may only be the 22nd-largest city in the US in size, but in historical legacy Boston is huge. Among the lofty phrases coined to describe the city are the 'Cradle of Liberty', the 'Athens of America', and 'the Hub of the Universe' (a variant of the latter was first used by one of Boston's greatest literary sons Oliver Wendell Holmes to describe the State House).

## A rich heritage

Many visitors come here to walk in the footsteps of the Founding Fathers and soak up the Old World atmosphere that nurtured some of America's most gifted artistic, mercantile, and political talents, including the poet Henry Wadsworth Longfellow (1807–82), the artist John Singer Sargent (1856–1925), and President John F. Kennedy (1917–63). Boston plays up this rich heritage in projects such as the Freedom Trail *(see p.25)*, the Black Heritage Trail *(see feature, p.53)*, and the Battle Road Trail *(see p.85)* between Lexington and Concord. That many historical monuments and sites have been preserved as part of the fabric of the city is a large part of Boston's appeal.

## HARBOR CITY

Boston's fortunes first came from its harbor, and this was a pivotal part of the city up until the early 20th century. With the end of the Big Dig *(see feature, p.13)* and the city's promotion of the HarborWalk route *(see p.75)*, attention is now flowing back to the long-neglected seashore. From May to mid-October you can take public ferries out to some of the 34 islands that are one of the city's biggest, yet least-known, natural assets *(see p.76)*. Another is its Emerald Necklace of parks and gardens *(see margin, left)* – Boston is one of America's greenest cities.

## TWO CITIES IN ONE

The graceful Charles River splits Boston to the south from the separate city of Cambridge, home to the Ivy League institutions Harvard and MIT, to the north. For all practical purposes the two cities interact as one, and Boston's efficient, clean, and safe subway system (known simply as the 'T') makes shuttling between the two sides a breeze. Walkers and cyclists can also make use of dedicated paths traversing eight bridges between Harvard and the river's mouth into the harbor.

**Emerald Necklace**
The Emerald Necklace – a corridor of interlinked parklands and gardens stretching for 7 miles (11km) from Boston Common to Franklin Park – was designed by Frederick Law Olmsted (1822–1903). He also conceived the beautiful Esplanade park that hugs the south bank of the Charles River, but which was not built until the 1930s, and New York's Central Park.

**Historic landmarks**
The US National Parks Service records 183 National Historic Landmarks in the state of Massachusetts; only New York state beats it with 257. A good proportion of these sites are found in the Boston city area and surrounding towns such as Concord, Lexington, Plymouth, Provincetown, and Salem.

## SEAT OF LEARNING

Spreading out from this central neighborhood is Greater Boston, which consists of nearly 100 towns with a total population of about 4.5 million. A not insignificant portion of that number is made up of young people who flock to the area's multiple seats of higher education, of which Harvard and MIT are but the cream of the crop. Boston University alone – its campus dominating the area around Commonwealth Avenue west of Kenmore Square – has 30,000 students enrolled. All this adds up to a liberal and vibrant atmosphere for a city that respects its past, but also has one foot striding into the future.

## ETHNIC DIVERSITY

The Boston area has long been a magnet for immigrants. The community most associated with the city are the Irish: they currently make up about 16 per cent of the population and remain the largest ethnic group, with a strong cultural influence in areas such as Jamaica Plain and South Boston. The Italian community, most visible in the North End *(see p.32)*, has given the city its current mayor, Thomas Menino – a popular politician and the first non-Irish mayor since 1884. Rounding out the city's ethnic diversity are more recent immigrants from Brazil, Vietnam, and China.

*Boston Brahmins*
For all this multiculturalism, Boston remains best-known for its Brahmins – the blue-blooded stock who can trace their ancestry back to the original 17th-century inhabitants of Massachusetts Bay Colony. Thanks to the philanthropic inclinations of many old Bostonian families, the city can share with one and all a treasure trove of art and culture, such as that on display at the wonderful Museum of Fine Arts *(see p.64)*. If this is what you are interested in, then a trip to nearby Salem *(see p.78)* to view the equally impressive collections of the Peabody Essex Museum is also recommended.

Above from far left: playing chess in Harvard Square; Boston skyline; canine Red Sox fan.

Below: students outside Harvard's Biological Laboratories.

Above from left: the Christian Science Plaza was designed by I.M. Pei; Public Garden in fall; Old State House.

## ARCHITECTURAL DEVELOPMENT

What comes to mind when most people think of Boston's architecture are red-brick terrace houses and the golden dome of the State House. People used to the strict grid plan of other American cities are also wrong-footed by the meandering roads of its more historical areas, such as Downtown, the North End, and Charlestown. However, over the four centuries since it was settled, much has changed in Boston's built landscape, and, like any dynamic city, it is still evolving.

### The colonial era

Not much from the earliest colonial period is left in Boston, mainly

Below: State House.

because the predominantly wooden houses of those days fell victim to frequent fires. Even as late as 1872 Boston was suffering catastrophic blazes: the Great Fire of that year wiped out most of the city center. The sole wooden construction from the 17th century that remains in central Boston is the Paul Revere House *(see p.33)* built in 1680. The city burghers learned their lesson from these conflagrations and ditched wood in favor of brick and stone. Note the contrast between the Tudor-style Revere House and its brick-built neighbor the Pierce-Hichborn House from 1711, a classic example of Georgian architecture along with the Old State House *(see p.29)*, dating from 1713.

### The 18th and 19th centuries

The architect most associated with Boston is Charles Bulfinch (1763–1844). The scion of a wealthy family, he traveled Europe soaking up ideas and influences that he later translated into the designs of friends' houses in Beacon Hill *(see pp.51, 52, and 55)*. The success of the homes led to Bulfinch being commissioned to design the new State House *(see p.51)* in 1798, which was something of a dry run for his US Capitol Building in Washington, DC.

By the early decades of the 19th century, land-reclamation projects were changing the shape of the city. Where the handsome terraces and garden squares of the South End *(see p.68)* and the grand mansions and boulevards of Back Bay *(see p.56)* now stand was once sea water and swamp. Boston's accumu-

lated wealth and culture is reflected in the elaborate buildings from this era, such as the Ames-Webster Mansion, built in 1872, and the even more flamboyant Burrage House (1889).

Italian Renaissance, neo-Gothic, and neo-Romanesque styles were all the rage. You can spot all these motifs around Copley Square, which is crowned by the Boston Public Library *(see p. 59)*, designed by Charles McKim (1847–1909) and one of the city's most impressive public buildings. Facing the library is Trinity Church, a masterpiece by Henry Hobson Richardson (1838–86), another great American architect.

## The 20th century

Boston got its first skyscraper in 1915, but high-rise buildings never really caught on here. The Prudential Tower (1965) and John Hancock Tower (1975) stand out mainly because there are so few other skyscrapers in the city. Boston's style of contemporary inner-city regeneration has, instead, been on a more human scale. First came the demolition of the old West End and construction of Government Center – a not entirely harmonious project that is softened by the success of the nearby Faneuil Hall-Quincy Market complex. Rising real-estate prices helped revive Back Bay and later the South End, both of which fell into decline in the middle of the 20th century.

## The 21st century

The completion of the massive engineering project known as the Big Dig *(see feature, below)* has reconnected the city with the harbor, enabling the focus to shift to the South Boston Seaport district. Here you will find the Institute of Contemporary Art *(see p. 75)*, which, along with the Frank Gehry-designed Stata Center *(see p. 48)* over in the Massachusetts Institute of Technology (MIT), is a contemporary example of the cutting-edge architecture that Boston has dabbled in right through its history. The Foster + Partners' Art of the Americas Wing at the Museum of Fine Arts and Renzo Piano's addition to the Isabella Stewart Gardner Museum *(see p. 66)* are lessons in how to harmoniously integrate new architecture with beloved classics.

### Boston lingo

Native Bostonians have a distinctive way of talking. The accent tends to result in an elongated 'a' and elided 'r' – hence 'Hahvahd Yahd', rather than Harvard Yard. Once you have got used to that, memorize the following commonly used shorthand to some of the city's locations: Com Ave – Commonwealth Avenue; JP – Jamaica Plain; Mass Ave – Massachusetts Avenue; Mem Drive – Memorial Drive; The Pike – The Massachusetts Turnpike.

## The end of the 'Big Dig'

The project to bury the Central Artery – the raised highway that sliced the harbor off from the Downtown area – in a tunnel beneath the city was known as the Big Dig. It took over a decade to complete, causing massive disruption, and cost in excess of $15 billion, making it one of the most expensive and controversial American civil engineering projects of recent times. The results, though, have widely been welcomed. Traffic flows much more freely across the city now, and the harbor and previously cut-off neighborhoods such as the North End are directly accessible via a pleasant strip of parkland known as the Rose F Kennedy Greenway. The highway emerges from its tunnel to cross the spectacular Leonard P. Zakim Bridge *(pictured)*, named after a local civil-rights activist.

# FOOD AND DRINK

*Once famous for its baked beans and meat-and-two-veg dinners, Boston cuisine today is equal parts traditional and contemporary. Beer is taken seriously, but there are also cool cocktail bars and hip cafés in which to relax.*

**Why Beantown?**
Back in the 18th century Boston was awash with molasses shipped in from the Caribbean as part of the rum trade. These were mixed with salt pork and beans to make baked beans, once the quint-essential Boston dish – hence the nickname Beantown. These days baked beans are not a common menu item; if you fancy trying them, Union Oyster House *(see p.31)* and Durgin Park *(see p.31)* both serve the dish.

## LOCAL SPECIALTIES

New England cooking is all about tra-ditional American produce, such as cranberries, corn, and seafood. Local specialties include creamy clam chow-der, scrod (small, tender haddock or cod) and steamers (clams with broth and butter). Be sure to sample at least one lobster roll – a soft-bread roll sandwich stuffed with lobster meat typically mixed with mayonnaise.

As you would expect for somewhere on the coast, you will find plenty of this style of cuisine in Boston itself, much of it excellent.

## HUMBLE TO HIGH-CLASS

Some of the city's best dining experi-ences are in the humblest of joints, be it enjoying a hearty breakfast or sand-wich at Charlie's Sandwich Shoppe *(see p.68)* or simply delicious fish and chips at The Daily Catch *(see p.33)*. That said, Boston also has a well-deserved reputation for contemporary American dining, as practiced by celebrity chefs such as Ken Oringer, of Clio and La Verdad Taqueria *(see pp.111 and 62)*, Todd English of Figs *(see p.39)*, and Barbara Lynch of No. 9 Park *(see p.117)* and Sportello *(see p.74)*.

**Right:** Hood (a home-grown dairy business) Milk Bottle; beer and burger.

## ETHNIC AND TRENDY

Boston's diverse immigrant population has bequeathed it a fine range of ethnic restaurants.

Chinatown is primarily packed with – you guessed it – Chinese restaurants, but it also has a smattering of Malaysian, Vietnamese, and Japanese eateries too.

The North End's vibe is almost exclusively Italian – from simple red-and-white-tablecloth cafés to sleek temples to regional *cucine*. For the trendiest dining spots, the South End and its SoWa (South of Washington) district are the places to head – between Tremont Street and Washington Avenue you will never go hungry.

Seafood, naturally, is a big feature of the Waterfront and up-and-coming Fort Point Channel areas, while the academic areas around Harvard and MIT are prime hunting grounds for good-value, atmospherically vibrant, and cosmopolitan restaurants and cafés. Cambridge's reputation for healthy organic cooking is deserved, but the town is also no slouch at fine dining. When it comes to discovering hot new chefs, it is this side of the Charles River that often proves the more fertile.

## BARS

The immigrant community most associated with Boston is that from Ireland. It should come as no surprise then that Irish bars seem to be located on every other corner of the city. A few are authentic, and worth visiting for a pint

or two *(see pp.120–2 for recommendations)*; others are kitsch tourist traps and best avoided.

Hip cocktail bars are also catching on, but Boston is too small a town to generate the kind of happening scene you would find in New York or London.

## CAFÉS

It is hard to beat the North End's collection of cafés for an espresso or cappuccino, but gourmet coffee can also be had beside Boston Common at Thinking Cup *(see p.28)* or in the South End at the South End Buttery *(see p.71)*. Tea-lovers will be heartened to know that the city's reputation for dumping the leaf in the harbor has been overturned at Tealuxe (0 Brattle Street; www.tealuxe.com) in Harvard.

Above from far left: freshly cooked lobster; Union Oyster House.

**Reservations**
Boston is not New York, so scoring a table at even the hottest places is well within the reach of ordinary mortals. Nevertheless, you would be well advised to make an advance booking for Friday or Saturday nights: try the online booking service www.open table.com. Note that some places do not take reservations at all, so turn up early or be prepared to wait.

# Beer city

Founding father Samuel Adams was a brewmaster, which explains why Boston's principal brewery adopted his name. Having started out as a micro-brewery in 1985, Sam Adams (www.samueladams.com) now produces a fine range of ales found in bars across the city. Micro-breweries that have stayed truly micro include Boston Beer Works (www.beerworks.net), which has branches near Fenway Park and the North End, John Harvard's Brew House (www.johnharvards.com) near Harvard Square, and Cambridge Brewing Company (www.cambrew.com) near MIT, Bukowski Tavern (bukowskitavern.net) in Back Bay and Cambridge stocks over 100 different brews.

# SHOPPING

*Boston's shopping does not stop at Red Sox souvenirs or a sweatshirt from Harvard or MIT. While tourists flock to the retail hubs of Faneuil Hall-Quincy Market and Newbury Street, do not miss the variety of shops that are tucked away in the South End and the side streets of Harvard.*

## Opening times
Most stores open Mon–Sat 9am–7pm, and shopping malls generally stay open until 9pm. On Sunday opening hours are typically noon–5pm or 6pm. Many smaller, independently owned shops and Downtown businesses are closed on Sunday.

## Sales taxes
All purchases, except unprepared food and clothing less than $175 per item, are subject to 6.25 per cent state sales tax. Clothing over $175 is taxed on the excess amount. Accessories (including shoes and bags) are subject to the tax.

Boston's shopping comes in very manageable chunks. While the obvious places to head for Red Sox souvenirs and the like are beside Fenway Park and the tourist magnet of Faneuil Hall-Quincy Market, those in search of less ubiquitous Boston products will not come away empty-handed.

### BACK BAY

The best range of shops is found around Back Bay. Newbury Street, often referred to as Boston's Rodeo Drive, offers the nicest retail experience and is renowned for its boutiques, art galleries, and quirky stores, particularly at the Massachusetts Avenue end. Riccardi (no. 116; www.riccardiboston.com) caters to the hip crowd, with fashions fresh off the runway. Root around The Closet (No. 175) for bargains on pre-loved high-end garments. John Fluevog (no. 302; www.fluevog.com) carries enough trendy shoes to satisfy even Imelda Marcos, while Johnny Cupcakes (no. 279; www.johnnycupcakes.com) and Life is Good (No. 283; www.lifeisgood.com) is the place for kooky cool T-shirts. Shreve, Crump & Low (www.shrevecrumpandlow.com), Boston's answer to Tiffany's, also has a new home at 39 Newbury St.

### THE MALLS

Since the closure of its downtown crossing location, Boston's main branch of bargain-hunters' store Filene's Basement (www.filenesbasement.com) is found at 497 Boylston Street. Further along Boylston, the foot of the Prudential Tower is surrounded by the Prudential Center shopping mall (www.prudentialcenter.com; *see p.60*). This is connected via an enclosed footbridge to another mall, ritzy Copley Place (www.simon.com), where you will find Barneys, selling up-and-coming designers, and the fancy department store Neiman Marcus. Across the Charles River Cambridgeside Galleria (www.cambridgesidegalleria.com), on Walk 4 or easily accessed from Lechmere T station offers up around 120 brand-name stores in one location.

### THE SOUTH END

One shopping area often overlooked by visitors is the South End. It is dotted with interesting independent shops and is a haven for art-lovers and epicureans. The epicenter of Boston's commercial contemporary art scene is Harrison Avenue *(see p.71)*. Here, Bernard Toale Gallery (at no. 450;

www.bernardtoalegallery.com) has long been known for representing Boston's emerging talent. Next door, Bobbie From Boston carries an impressive collection of vintage garments; designers from Ralph Lauren shop here for inspiration.

For modern design homewares, visit Lekker (www.lekkerhome.com), on the corner of Washington and Waltham streets, and Hudson (www.hudson-boston.com) at 12 Union Park Street. Tucked away in a courtyard at 46 Waltham Street is Patch NYC (www.patchnyc.com) stocking gifts and decorative arts. Around the block on Shawmut Avenue, Michele Mercaldo (no. 276; michelemercaldo.com) offers one-of-a-kind fine jewelry. Boston's best deli, South End Formaggio (no. 268; southendformaggio.com) offers free wine-and-cheese tastings.

## HARVARD SQUARE

Over in Cambridge, despite many chain stores moving in, Harvard Square still maintains an academic atmosphere, with J. August (1320 Massachusetts Avenue) and the Harvard Coop (Harvard Square) overflowing with Harvard insignia on everything. If the Coop does not stock the book you are after, chances are you will find it at one of several other bookstores in the area, including Harvard Bookstore (1256 Massachusetts Avenue www.harvard.com), specializing in used and remainders; Grolier (6 Plympton Street), offering America's largest poetry selection; and Schoenhof's For-

eign Books (76A Mount Auburn Street www.schoenhofs.com); and the children's bookstore Curious George Goes to Wordsworth (1 John F. Kennedy Street). Browsing the Museum of Useful Things on the corner of John F. Kennedy and Brattle streets is sure to turn up that useful something you never knew you needed.

## DOWNTOWN AND FORT POINT

Downtown Crossing's shopping is pretty much limited to Macy's and a few specialty stores such as Bromfield Camera (10 Bromfield Street; www.bromfieldcamera.com) which has been serving photographers since 1965.

Unsurprisingly, tourists love Faneuil Hall-Quincy Market (*see pp.30 and 72;* www.faneuilhallmarketplace.com), with over 100 local and national name stores gathered here. Check out Boston Pewter Company (www.bostonpewtercompany.com) in the basement of Faneuil Hall, or the Revolutionary Boston Museum Shop in Quincy Market. Fort Point shopping took a major leap forward with the relocation of designer store Louis-Boston (www.louisboston.com) to Fan Pier. The arts and crafts of the many artists who work and live in the area can be found at Made in Fort Point (12 Farnsworth Street) and the gallery FP3 (346 Congress Street; www.fp3boston.com). The shop at the ICA *(see p.75)* is also worth a look for art books, objets d'art, and contemporary jewelry.

**Above from far left:**
Faneuil Hall Marketplace; kitted out in Red Sox gear; designer fashions on Newbury Street; Harvard is the place for books.

**Beacon Hill**
This neighborhood is known for tradition and history, so it is no surprise that over 40 antiques shops have congregated here on Charles Street. Judith Dowling Asian Art at (no. 133; judithdowling.com) specializes in Japanese decorative arts and functional objects; Eugene Galleries at (no. 76; eugenegalleries.com) offers fine prints, etchings, and old maps, while E.R. Butler & Co. (no. 38; www.erbutler.com) carries distinctive hardware and tableware inspired by historical designs.

# SPORTS AND ENTERTAINMENT

*Baseball is king in Boston, with a city-wide devotion to the Red Sox, even though other sports teams are national champs too. The youthful student population also makes this a great place to party, with a diverse range of musical and theatrical offerings every night of the week.*

**Basketball champs**
For all the hoopla over the Red Sox, it is the Celtics who are the most successful team in any major sport in the country. Beginning in 1959, they won an unprecedented eight National Basketball Association (NBA) championships on the trot, and to date have 17 NBA wins to their credit.

**Listings**
Pick up a free copy of either *The Phoenix* (thephoenix.com) or *Weekly Dig* (digboston.com) to see who and what is playing around town, as well as for the low-down on the hottest clubs.

**Right:** Red Sox programs outside Fenway Park.

## BASEBALL

Sports run in Boston's blood, none more so than the Red Sox (boston. redsox.mlb.com). In 2004 the city's Major League Baseball team finally broke the losing 'curse' in the World Series championships that had haunted them for 86 years – ever since the legendary slugger Babe Ruth was sold to eternal rivals, the New York Yankees. To prove their new-found form, the Red Sox snatched another World Series victory in 2007, much to the delight of Bostonians, who turned out en masse to welcome their heroes home in a tickertape parade.

## OTHER SPORTS

The Red Sox can now stand proudly shoulder to shoulder with the city's American football team, the New England Patriots (www.patriots.com). One of the most successful teams in NFL history, the 'Pats' are three-time winners of the Super Bowl. Their home ground is the Gillette Stadium at Foxborough, 22 miles (35km) south of Boston, and the season runs from late August to late December.

From October to mid-April at the TD Garden Stadium (on Causeway Street above North Station), you can catch the games of the city's ice hockey team, the Bruins (bruins.nhl.com), or the basketball team, the Celtics (www.nba.com/celtics).

## CLASSICAL MUSIC, OPERA, AND BALLET

Offering everything from garage-band rock to orchestral works, Boston is one of the US's most musically diverse cities. For classical music, check out the concert schedule of the beautiful Symphony Hall (301 Massachusetts Avenue; tel: 617-266-1200; www.bso.org), which

hosts the world-class Boston Symphony Orchestra, founded in 1881, from November to May; the orchestra can also be heard occasionally playing outdoors at the Hatch Shell in the Esplanade *(see p.49)*, where you may also catch the Symphony's spin-off Boston Pops Orchestra. Another excellent venue is Jordan Hall at the New England Conservatory of Music (30 Gainsborough Street; tel: 617-585-1260; necmusic.edu), which stages many free concerts alongside ones by established ensembles, such as the Boston Philharmonic (www.bostonphil.org).

Opera, not Boston's strong point, is covered by the Boston Lyric Opera (blo.org) and the Boston Opera (www.operaboston.org). However, the Boston Ballet (bostonballet.org) is considered one of the top dance companies in the US.

## ROCK AND POP

The stars of rock and pop regularly turn up at the city's biggest venues, such as the outdoor Bank of America Pavilion (May–Sept only) out on South Boston Waterfront, and T.D. Banknorth Garden (www.tdbanknorthgarden. com), or medium-sized spaces such as House of Blues (15 Landsdowne Street; www.houseofblues.com) or the Orpheum Theater (1 Hamilton Place; www.orpheum-theater.com). However, with all those students around, there is an enormous range of small live music venues and a thriving indie rock scene of bands and singers to fill them. Check out places such as T.T. the Bear's Place

and Paradise Rock Club *(see pp.120–3 for nightlife listings).*

## THEATER SCENE

Boston has a small but lively theater scene, with the city's grandest theaters, such as the Wang and the Shubert, often used for try-outs of Broadway-bound productions. The city's equivalent of *The Mousetrap* is the comic whodunnit *Shear Madness* (www.shearmadness.com), staged since 1980 at the Charles Playhouse (74 Warrenton Street; www.blue man.com), where you can also catch the long-running Blue Man Group.

The most reliable places for interesting productions are The American Repertory Theatre (Loeb Drama Center, 64 Brattle Street; www.amer icanrepertorytheater.org) over in Harvard, the Huntington (www.hunt ingtontheatre.org), and the South End's Boston Center for the Arts (www.bcaonline.org), which has four stages *(see p.71).*

## The Boston Marathon

Since 1897, Patriot's Day – the third Monday in April – has seen city traffic come to a standstill for the running of the Boston Marathon (www.baa.org), making this the world's oldest annually contested long-distance running race. That first 26-mile (42km) race began with just 15 participants, but today the marathon regularly has over 30,000 runners, including Olympic champions. The toughest section is the aptly named Heartbreak Hill, which rises up 80ft (24.3m) in the city's Newton Hills area. A half-marathon held in early October attracts around 5,000 runners.

# HISTORY: KEY DATES

*Settled by Native Americans for thousands of years before John Cabot claimed Massachusetts for King Henry VII of England in 1497, the Boston area is famous for its key role in American Independence.*

## PRE-REVOLUTIONARY BOSTON

**Below:** stained-glass window in the State House commemorating 1775; statue of Washington, the first president, in the Public Garden *(see p.55)*; detail from the Shaw-54th Regiment Memorial, honoring the first regiment of freed blacks in the Civil War *(see p.50)*.

| | |
|---|---|
| **1625** | William Blackstone, Boston's first colonist, settles on the Common. |
| **1630** | Puritan English settlers led by John Winthrop form Massachusetts Bay Company colony at Charlestown. |
| **1635** | Boston Latin School, the first public school in the nation, is founded. |
| **1636** | Harvard College is founded. |
| **1684** | Massachusetts Bay Company is made into a royal colony with a governor appointed by the king. |
| **1692** | The Salem Witch Trials begin. |
| **1761** | Boston lawyer James Otis declares: 'Taxation without representation is tyranny.' |
| **1764** | The Sugar Act and the Stamp Act arouse anti-royalist sentiments. |

## THE BATTLE FOR INDEPENDENCE

| | |
|---|---|
| **1770** | Boston Massacre. |
| **1773** | Boston Tea Party. |
| **1775** | Paul Revere's ride and battles of Lexington and Concord spark the American Revolution. Battle of Bunker Hill and burning of Charlestown. George Washington takes command of Continental Army at Cambridge. |
| **1776** | British troops withdraw from Massachusetts. Declaration of Independence is announced from State House. |
| **1789** | US Constitution is framed; John Hancock is declared first governor of state of Massachusetts. |
| **1795** | Paul Revere and Samuel Adams lay the cornerstone for the new State House designed by Charles Bulfinch on Beacon Hill. |

## 19TH CENTURY

| | |
|---|---|
| **1812** | War of 1812 against the British paralyzes the city's commerce. |
| **1821** | English High School, the first high school in the US, is opened. |
| **1822** | Boston is finally incorporated as a city. |
| **1841** | First Irish immigrants arrive. |

| 1852 | Charles McKim's Boston Public Library opens. |
|---|---|
| 1857 | Filling of Back Bay begins. |
| 1861 | Massachusetts Institute of Technology (MIT) granted charter. |
| 1861–5 | American Civil War. |
| 1872 | Great Fire of Boston. |
| 1876 | Salem resident Alexander Graham Bell patents the telephone. |
| 1879 | Mary Baker Eddy founds the Christian Science Church. |
| 1881 | Boston Symphony Orchestra is founded. Frederick Law Olmsted, landscape architect, begins work on Emerald Necklace park system. |
| 1897 | First Boston Marathon. America's first subway opens at Park Street. |

## 20TH CENTURY

| 1903 | Boston is the site of first World Series – Red Sox win. First international wireless message transmitted from Wellfleet on Cape Cod. |
|---|---|
| 1910 | A dam is built to form the Charles River Basin. |
| 1915 | Boston's first skyscraper is built. |
| 1919 | Strike of 1,300 Boston police. Breaking it brings to national prominence Massachusetts Governor Calvin Coolidge. |
| 1946 | John Fitzgerald Kennedy is elected Congressman for Charlestown and Cambridge. |
| 1957 | Boston Redevelopment Authority is launched by Mayor John Hynes. |
| 1968 | Completion of new City Hall. |
| 1980s | The 'Massachusetts Miracle' high-tech revolution results in an economic boom. |
| 1990 | Thieves remove $200 million in paintings from Isabella Stewart Gardner Museum in the largest art heist in history. |
| 1991 | Start of the 'Big Dig' civic reconstruction. |
| 1996 | The Harbor Islands are designated a national park area. |

## 21ST CENTURY

| 2004 | The Red Sox break 87-year losing streak by winning World Series. The US's first legally recognized same-sex wedding takes place in Cambridge. Harvard students set up social networking site Facebook. |
|---|---|
| 2007 | The 'Big Dig' is finally fully completed. |
| 2008 | Boston Celtics win the NBA championships for the 17th time. |
| 2009 | Thomas Menino secures a fifth term of office, becoming Boston's longest serving mayor. |
| 2012 | Opening of Renzo Piano-designed new entrance and wing to the Isabella Stewart Gardner Museum. |

# WALKS AND TOURS

# BOSTON COMMON AND DOWNTOWN

*Covering the first half of the historic Freedom Trail, this route runs from Boston Common, the city's geographical and social crossroads, through Downtown, to the oldest continuously run restaurant in the US.*

**Visitor information**
Boston's main Visitor Information Center (tel: 617-536-4100; www.bostonusa.com; daily 8.30am–5pm) is located on the northeastern edge of Boston Common, just south of the Park Street subway station (corner of Park and Tremont streets). You can pick up free maps and book tours here. It also serves as the beginning of the Freedom Trail *(see opposite).*

**DISTANCE** 1½ miles (2.5km)
**TIME** A half day
**START** Boylston T Station
**END** Haymarket T Station
**POINTS TO NOTE**

Downtown is busy with office workers Monday to Friday, particularly around lunchtime, so a good time to do this walk is early morning after rush hour or at the weekend. On Friday and Saturday there is also a lively fresh-produce market at Haymarket. If you do the walk in the afternoon, you could finish with dinner in Chinatown and a show in the Theater District.

Starting at Boston Common, one of the oldest sections of the city, and ending at the cobblestone streets of Blackstone Block, this walk will take you deep into Boston's history. During its 360-plus years the Common has been a popular spot for sermons, promenades, and, in the years before the Revolution, political protest. Stroll through it today and you will see everyone from Chinese women practicing t'ai chi in the shade of ancient elm trees to rappers and breakdancers showing off their skills, and office workers from Downtown's modern skyscrapers grabbing some fresh air while enjoying their lunch.

## Chinatown and Theater District

Close to the walk's start, immediately east of Bolyston Street, are Boston's Chinatown and Theater District, areas you will likely want to return to for dining and evening entertainment. At the intersection of Surface Road and Beach Street (Chinatown's main drag) is an ornate *paifang*, a traditional-style Chinese gateway flanked by a pair of stone foo lions. The area around it has recently been landscaped into an attractive garden with bamboo and water features – a result of Downtown beautification after the Big Dig *(see p.13)*. Chinatown might not be large, but it is packed with lively Asian restaurants and exotic stores. It is great fun to visit, and can easily be combined with a night out at one of the theaters on Stuart or Tremont streets, such as the Wang and Shubert, where for decades Broadway-bound productions have had their trial runs.

**Below:** for dim sum head to Chinatown.

### The Freedom Trail

Most of this route follows a section of the 2½-mile (4km) Freedom Trail. This runs through the heart of Boston past 16 significant sites that are among the city's oldest landmarks and featured in the decisive break that New England's settlers made from the British in 1776. Established in 1958 to preserve these key monuments and sites, the Trail is marked by a red-brick or painted line on the pavement. It is relatively easy to follow, but if you would prefer, **The Freedom Trail Foundation** (tel: 617-357-8300; www.thefreedomtrail.org) offers daily guided tours from the Visitor Information Center *(see margin, left)* or Faneuil Hall *(see p.30)*.

### BOSTON COMMON

This walk starts at the southeast corner of **Boston Common**, at the junction of Boylston and Tremont streets. The Common, established in 1634, is the oldest public park in the US and a storybook of Boston history. Originally used as a 'Comon Field' *(sic)* on which sheep and cattle grazed (they did so up until 1830), the pentagonal space, covering about 50 acres (20 hectares), was also used as a mustering ground for militias and a venue for public hangings. Among those who met a cruel end dangling from the Great Elm, which stood on the Common until 1876, was Mary Dyer, the heroic Quaker who insisted on the right to worship freely. A statue in her memory stands outside the State House on the corner of Beacon and Bowdon streets *(see margin, p.51)*.

### Central Burying Ground

Immediately to the left as you face the Common from the corner of Boylston Street is the **Central Burying Ground ❶** (daily dawn–dusk). During the American Revolution the Common was transformed into a British military center. As many as 2,000 Redcoats were quartered here during Boston's occupation, and several dozen British

Above from far left: shady spot on Boston Common; Freedom Trail pavement sign; tour guide in period costume; Cutler Majestic Theatre in the Theater District.

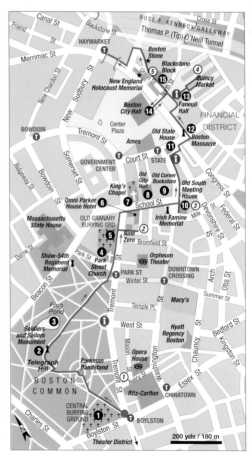

### Free Shakespeare

A midsummer tradition is the Free Shakespeare on the Common, with performances held on Boston Common from mid-July to early August. See www.commshakes. org for details.

soldiers killed at the Battle of Bunker Hill were interred in the cemetery. It is the city's fourth-oldest cemetery, but few of note are buried here. One exception is Gilbert Stuart (1755–1828) who painted the classic portrait of George Washington *(see p.65)*.

### Soldiers and Sailors Monument

The western part of the Common is devoted to athletic endeavor, with a well-patronized baseball field and tennis courts. Head north from the burying ground, watching out for scampering grey squirrels, past the pretty Parkman Bandstand, to admire the 70ft (21m) **Soldiers and Sailors Monument ❷**, located atop Telegraph Hill. It is dedicated to the Union forces killed in the Civil War.

### Frog Pond

Close by is **Frog Pond ❸**, used as a children's wading pool in summer and an ice rink in winter. In colonial times

sheep and cows slaked their thirst at this watering hole. Later, Bostonians fished in it for minnows in the summer and ice-skated on it in the winter, and here they celebrated the first arrival of piped-in municipal water from a suburban reservoir in 1848. Sadly, lined with concrete today, the pond is no longer a home for minnows nor frogs.

### PARK STREET

Exit the Common at its northeast corner on Park Street. If you fancy refreshments at this point, you can backtrack down Tremont Street Street to find **Thinking Cup**, see ⓧⓘ.

Just north of Park Street T Station, on the corner of Park and Tremont streets, stands **Park Street Church ❹** (tel: 617-523-3383; www.parkstreet. org; mid-June–Aug Tue–Fri 9am–4pm, Sat 9am–3pm free), with its majestic 217ft (66m) steeple (adapted from a Christopher Wren design). William Lloyd Garrison delivered his first anti-slavery speech here in 1829.

### OLD GRANARY BURYING GROUND

Next to the church, on Tremont Street, pay your respects at the grave of Paul Revere, Samuel Adams, John Hancock, and other key revolutionary figures in the illustrious **Old Granary Burying Ground ❺** (9am–5pm, winter until 3pm), dating from 1660. The graveyard is named after the granary that was demolished to make way for the Park Street Church.

## Taking a trolley

Several sightseeing 'trolleys' (in fact, conventional wheeled vehicles with trolley-like bodywork) run at roughly 15-minute intervals on routes around Boston's main sights. It is a great way to see the city, especially if time is limited. You can hop off wherever you like, explore on foot, and then board a later trolley – just make sure the trolley company matches your ticket. Operators include

Old Town Trolley Tours (tel: 888-910-8687; www.trolleytours.com/Boston), City View Trolley Tours (tel: 617-363-7899; www.city viewtrolleys.com), and Brush Hill Tours (tel: 800-343-1328; www.brushhilltours.com).

Opposite is Bosworth St at the end of which is the sandwich shop **Sam La Grassa's**, see ⑪②.

## OMNI PARKER HOUSE HOTEL

Return to Tremont St and continue to the corner with School, past the fancy Venetian facade of the Tremont Temple Baptist Church (once a famous Boston theater), where stands the **Omni Parker House Hotel** ❻, the oldest continuously operating hotel in the US. The present building is not the original, but much of the lobby's ornately carved wooden decoration is. Pop inside to see where Charles Dickens conducted literary seminars, the Vietnamese leader Ho Chi Minh waited on tables, and Malcolm X toiled in the kitchen. The hotel lays claim to inventing a couple of Boston's culinary favourites – Boston cream pie and the Parker Roll, a soft bread roll.

## KING'S CHAPEL AND BURYING GROUND

On the corner of School and Tremont streets is **King's Chapel** ❼ (tel: 617-227-2155; www.kings-chapel.org; July–Aug daily 10am–4pm, other months Sat 10am–4pm, Sun 1.30–4pm; services Wed 12.15pm and Sun 11am). The present granite structure dates from 1754, but the chapel had its origins in the 1680s, when Britain's King James II made a colossal political blunder by sending to Boston a clergyman whose job was to install in the town the very thing the Puritans had hated and fled: a branch of the Church of England.

Next to the Chapel, on Tremont Street, is Boston's first cemetery, **King's Chapel Burying Ground** (daily 9am–5pm, winter until 3pm), in use from 1630 to 1796, thus predating the Anglican edifice whose name it later assumed. The Bay Colony's first

**Above from far left:**
Parkman Bandstand;
Omni Parker House
Hotel; King's Chapel
and Burying Ground.

**The historic T**
Opened in 1897,
'Park Street Under'
was the first subway
station in the US. The
subway now falls
under the auspices of
the Massachusetts
Bay Transport
Authority (MBTA;
see pp.104–6). Most
Bostonians simply
call it 'The T,' after
the system's logo:
a T in a circle.

**Below left:** Park
Street Church.

## Food and Drink 🍴

### ① THINKING CUP
165 Tremont St; tel: 617-482-5555; www.thinkingcup.com;
Mon–Wed 7am–10pm, Thur–Sun 7am–11pm; $
Trade up from Starbucks at this sophisticated self-serve café
serving much-praised Sumptown Coffee – they use only the
finest beans from around the world. Add in a pastry, baked
goodie, or sandwich and you're good to go.

### ② SAM LA GRASSA'S
44 Providence Street; tel: 617-357-6861;
www.samlagrassas.com; Mon–Fri 11am–3.30pm; $
The sliced meats and cheeses are piled high on the many cre-
ative sandwiches available at this very popular Downtown café;
signature sarnies include the Famous Rumanian Pastrami and
Pulled BBQ chicken. Salads and other treats are also available
and you can eat in or take away.

## Ticket saving

There is a combined discount ticket for visiting the Old South Meeting House and Paul Revere House *(see p.33)*, sold for $8 at both venues; it can be used any time. From April to November you can also buy the Freedom Trail Ticket ($13) which covers these two places and the Old State House.

**Below:** Old South Meeting House.

governor, John Winthrop, was buried here in 1649.

The monument at the corner of the burying ground honors a French naval adjutant, the Chevalier de Saint-Sauveur, killed by a Boston mob in September 1778 during an altercation over bread. The French, who had come to help the colonials, were baking bread using their own stores of wheat; Bostonians, who were enduring a severe shortage of flour, were incensed when told that they could not buy the French Navy's bread. The Chevalier's funeral service is said to have been the first Catholic Mass in Boston.

## OLD CITY HALL

Further down School Street is **Old City Hall ❽** (tel: 617-523-8678; www.oldcityhall.com), built in 1865 in the French Second Empire style. When the city government decamped from here in 1969 for the new City Hall *(see p.30)*, this handsome edifice was preserved as a mixed-use complex of offices and a steak restaurant.

In the forecourt are bronze statues of Benjamin Franklin and Josiah Quincy, in his time a senator, Boston mayor, and president of Harvard. Pop into the hall's vestibule to read about the building's history and that of the Boston Latin School, the nation's first school, which once stood close to this spot – hence the name School Street. Look down the sidewalk outside and you will see a pretty hopscotch mosaic celebrating the school.

## OLD CORNER BOOKSTORE

Continue to the intersection of School and Washington streets, where you will find the **Old Corner Bookstore ❾**, dating from 1712, and currently a jeweler's. Over the years the building has served as an apothecary, a dry-goods store, and private residence, although it is fondly remembered in its 1828 incarnation as the home of the eminent Ticknor and Fields publishing firm and a bookstore. In the Golden Age of American literature the store was a popular meeting place for Whittier, Emerson, Stowe, Alcott, and other distinguished writers.

In the small square opposite stands the **Irish Famine Memorial**, which honors the 37,000 Irish who emigrated to America in the mid-19th century in the wake of Ireland's potato famine.

## OLD SOUTH MEETING HOUSE

Immediately to the right on Washington Street is the **Old South Meeting House** ❿ (tel: 617-482-6439; www.oldsouthmeetinghouse.org; daily Apr–Oct 9.30am–5pm, Nov–Mar 10am–4pm; charge), built in 1727 and styled after the graceful London chapels of Sir Christopher Wren. The church was the scene of the events that preceded the infamous Boston Tea Party of 1773 and the baptism on a chilly January 6, 1706, of Benjamin Franklin, born around the corner on Milk Street, where you will find the **Milk Street Café**, see ⑪③.

## OLD STATE HOUSE

From the Old South Meeting House, continue north along Washington Street toward the junction with State Street. Immediately to the right, overshadowed by modern skyscrapers, is the **Old State House** ⓫ (tel: 617-720-1713; www.bostonhistory.org; daily 9am–5pm, Jan until 4pm, June–late Aug until 6pm; charge), Boston's oldest public building, built in 1713 as the seat of the colonial government. It now houses a small museum. In 1787 John Hancock was inaugurated here as the first governor of the state under its new Constitution. You can recognize the building by those symbols of British imperial power, the lion and unicorn, the originals of which were thrown into the street when the Declaration of Independence was read from the balcony on July 18, 1776. On display inside are items relating to Boston's role in the Revolutionary War and other parts of the city's history.

## BOSTON MASSACRE

Continuing along the Freedom Trail from the Old State House, it is easy to miss the circle of cobblestones on a tiny traffic island at the junction of State and Congress streets. This marks the spot of the **Boston Massacre** ⓬ where, on March 5, 1770, a handful of British soldiers fired into a jeering crowd that was pelting them with snowballs; five men were killed, including former slave Crispus Attucks, who is buried in the Old Granary Burying Ground *(see p.26)*.

**Above from far left:** guide in colonial dress; clock atop the Old State House; Irish Famine Memorial.

**Boston Tea Party**
It was on December 16, 1773, at the Old South Meeting House, that more than 5,000 Bostonians met to decide what to do with three tea-laden ships in the harbor. Disguised as Mohawk Indians, a gang of colonists, enraged at the British tax placed on tea and other imports, ran down Milk Street to Griffins Wharf. The crowd followed, and, with cries of 'Boston harbor a teapot tonight!', 340 crates of tea were dumped overboard.

### Food and Drink 🍴
**③ MILK STREET CAFÉ**
50 Milk Street; tel: 617-542-3663; milkstreetcafe.com; Mon–Fri 7am–3pm; $
Reasonable prices for generous portions is the deal at this kosher cafeteria, with dairy and fish, no meats. Find made-from-scratch dishes, such as roasted salmon salad and vegetable lasagne, and nutritious homemade soups.

**Below:** period outfit in the Old State House.

## FANEUIL HALL

Head north on Congress Street and turn right to reach **Faneuil Hall** ⑬ (www.faneuilhall.com; free). A statue of Samuel Adams, one of the Founding Fathers of the United States, stands in front this historic public hall, named after benefactor Peter Faneuil. Designated by patriot orator James Otis as the 'Cradle of Liberty,' it was here that the Sons of Liberty called many meetings of complaint about British taxation without representation.

The original hall was built in 1742; the current one was designed by Charles Bulfinch in 1805.

Recent renovations have seen the **National Park Service Visitor Center**

**Below:** Faneuil Hall.

(www.nps.gov/bost; daily 9am– 5pm) installed on the ground floor along with various shops. Come here for information and for Ranger-led free daily walking tours along part of the Freedom Trail; see the website for details. Upstairs, if a public meeting is not taking place, a ranger also conducts a history talk in the Great Hall (daily 9am–5pm; free).

In the adjacent Quincy Market complex, which is covered in walk 10 *(see p.72)*, you will find several places to eat, including **Durgin Park**, see ⑪④.

## BOSTON CITY HALL

On the western side of Congress Street, climb the concrete steps leading up to **Boston City Hall** ⑭. Prior to the construction in 1969 of this charmless inverted ziggurat, the area was known as Scollay Square, a slightly disreputable entertainment area. In the 1960s the Boston Redevelopment Authority decided to raze Scollay Square and the nearby tenements of the West End. The area was renamed Government Center, its focus the vast, empty, and depressing City Hall Plaza.

## NEW ENGLAND HOLOCAUST MEMORIAL

Also far from uplifting, but beautiful in a melancholy way, are the six tall, slender glass-and-steel towers of the **New England Holocaust Memorial** in Carmen Park, a strip of greenery

opposite the City Hall between Union and Congress streets. Forming a mute tribute to the those murdered by the Nazis in World War II, each glass column, wreathed in steam symbolizing the gas chambers, represents a different concentration camp and is inscribed with numbers – 6 million in total.

At the Faneuil Hall end of the park are two bronze statues of James Curley, the Irish politician who dominated Boston politics from 1920 to 1950, even managing to be re-elected while in jail.

## BLACKSTONE BLOCK

In stark contrast to the concrete wastelands of Government Center are the charming brick buildings and cobbled lanes, dating back to the 17th century, of **Blackstone Block ⓰**, named after Boston's first colonist, William Blackstone (who settled in the Boston Common area in 1625). The block is bounded by Union, Hanover, Blackstone, and North streets. At 41 Union Street is the historic **Union Oyster House**, see ⓸⓹.

A few yards down Marshall Street (just off Union Street), opposite the 18th-century Ebenezer Hancock House at no. 10, look down to see the **Boston Stone**, a stone ball and stone trough built into the wall of a gift shop. Shipped from England in 1700 to serve as a paint mill, the stones were later used as the point from which all distances from Boston were measured. Their role as the hub of

'The Hub' was later taken over by the dome of the Massachusetts State House *(see p.51)*.

If it is Friday or Saturday, you might want to linger around here to enjoy the **fresh produce market** that wraps its way around North and Blackstone streets.

Otherwise, return to Congress Street, at the head of which is **Haymarket Station**, where you can finish this tour, or catch the T back to Boylston or Chinatown stations for dinner and a night at the theater *(see p.24)*. Alternatively, continue across the Rose F. Kennedy Greenway into the North End for the second half of the Freedom Trail *(see p.32)*.

*(see p.51)*, *(see p.24)*, *(see p.32)*

---

## Food and Drink 🍴

### ④ DURGIN PARK

340 North Market, Faneuil Hall; tel: 617-227-2038; Mon–Sat 11.30am–10pm, Sun 11.30am–9pm; $$

Opened in 1827, Durgin Park still retains the same pressed-tin ceilings and mosaic-tile floor, as well as the same Yankee-style cooking (think shepherd's pie and homemade fish cakes), all of which is served at communal tables in huge portions.

### ⑤ UNION OYSTER HOUSE

41 Union Street; tel: 617-227-2750; www.unionoysterhouse.com; Sun–Thur 11am–9.30pm, Fri–Sat 11am–10pm; $$

A favorite haunt of President Kennedy, this touristy restaurant has a top-class raw bar, and serves both seafood and steaks in atmospheric rooms with creaky floors, low ceilings, and wooden booths.

---

**Above from far left:** stark Boston City Hall; seafood institution on Union Street; New England Holocaust Memorial.

**Ye olde house** Union Oyster House claims the title of Boston's oldest brick house. A rare example of Georgian architecture in the city, the restaurant dates from at least 1660, when it was owned by Boston's first town crier, William Courser. Mentioned in a city plan of 1708, the house was the office of the *Massachusetts Spy* newspaper from 1771 to 1775, while in 1796 the exiled Louis-Philippe, who later became king of France, taught French in the rooms above James Amblard's tailor shop.

# THE NORTH END AND CHARLESTOWN

*The second half of the Freedom Trail traverses the North End and Charlestown, two of Boston's oldest settled areas, packed with historical sites and great places to eat and drink. The North End, Boston's Little Italy, is an especially pleasant place to return to in the evening for a meal.*

**Above:** snapshots of Boston's Little Italy.

**DISTANCE** 2½ miles (4.5km)
**TIME** A half day
**START** Haymarket T Station
**END** Community College T Station
**POINTS TO NOTE**

This walk follows on from the end of walk 1, and the two can be linked for a full day's itinerary. An alternative way to access or leave this walk is by hopping on the Inner Harbor Ferry, which connects Charlestown Navy Yard with Long Wharf beside the Aquarium *(see p.74)*. Ferries run daily, every 30 minutes on the quarter of the hour, between 6.30am and 8pm, and cost $1.70.

Much of the North End's charm as a neighborhood comes from its improvisational quality, with a hodgepodge of buildings – some quite attractive, others not, and many dating from the late 1800s, when they were used as tenement houses for European immigrants.

Hanover Street is the area's main thoroughfare, but around it spreads an archaic and confusing street plan. The North End is one of those places where it is easy to get lost, and prob-ably best that you do. All kinds of unconventional spaces, not to mention many delicious delis, cafés, and restaurants can be discovered in the neighborhood's less traveled areas.

## ROSE F KENNEDY GREENWAY

Begin the walk at **Haymarket T Station**. Until only a few years ago the raised expanse of the Fitzgerald Expressway (also known as the Central Artery) cut the North End off from the rest of the city. Now that the Big Dig has buried the road underground *(see feature, p.13)*, the cleared land forms a ribbon of parks through the city, known collectively as the **Rose F Kennedy Greenway** (www.rosekennedygreenway.org). Rose Fitzgerald Kennedy, mother of President John F. Kennedy, was born in the North End in 1890, and her funeral was conducted at St Stephen's Church *(see p.34)* on Hanover Street in 1995.

## HANOVER STREET

Head southeast through the park until you reach Hanover Street. On either

side, as the street cuts through the park, are railings inscribed with historical dates and quotations about the area from past residents.

As Hanover Street enters the North End it is almost wall-to-wall with cafés and restaurants. For an espresso to power your way stop at **Caffé Paradiso**, see ⑪①. A bit further along the street, you will come to **Caffé Vittoria**, see ⑪②, and **The Daily Catch**, see ⑪③, which are both also recommended.

## Food and Drink 🍴

### ① CAFFÉ PARADISO

255 Hanover Street; tel: 617-742-1768; www.caffeparadiso.com; daily 7am–2am; $$

A popular local hangout, this café's espresso, cannoli, panini, and calzoni are particularly delicious. The TV beams in soccer games from Italy via satellite.

### ② CAFFÉ VITTORIA

290–296 Hanover Street; tel: 617-227-7606; www.vittoriacaffe.com; daily 7am–midnight; $

A quintessential Italian café, with quirky decor that includes almost a museum's worth of antique espresso machines. All kinds of other beverages are also served, along with traditional sweets.

### ③ THE DAILY CATCH

323 Hanover Street; tel: 617-523-8567; www.dailycatch.com; Sun–Thur 11am–10pm, Fri–Sat 11am–11pm; $

Cash only at this hole-in-the-wall institution that specializes in Sicilian seafood. The branch at Fan Pier, 2 Northern Avenue (tel: 617-772-4400), handy for walk 10 *(see p.74)*.

## PAUL REVERE HOUSE

Turn right on Richmond Street and then left to enter cobbled North Square, where at no. 19 you will find the **Paul Revere House** ❶ (tel: 617-523-2338; www.paulreverehouse.org; daily mid-Apr–Oct 9.30am–5.15pm, Nov–mid-Apr 9.30am–4.15pm, Jan–Mar closed

Above from far left: view of the North End from St Stephen's Church to the Old North Church; Paul Revere House; Italian fare abounds in the North End.

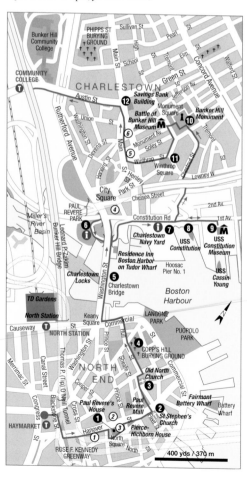

## Steeple lore

The Old North Church's 175ft (53m) steeple houses eight bells cast in 1744 in the UK – they are the oldest in the US and still rung nearly every Saturday morning. In April 1775, the sexton, on instructions from Paul Revere, hung two lanterns from the Old North Church steeple to warn that the British were advancing on Concord from Boston Common. In 1860, Longfellow climbed the steeple, which inspired him to write *Paul Revere's Ride*. Today's steeple is a 1955 reproduction. The original was destroyed by a hurricane in 1806, as was its replacement in 1954.

Mon charge). Built in 1680, this two-story dwelling, with an overhanging second floor, is downtown Boston's oldest wooden house. Revere, then a silversmith, took up residence in 1770, and the house is furnished today much as it was when it was home to him and the first Mrs Revere, who bore him eight children, and then, when she died, to the second Mrs Revere, who produced a similar brood. It is from here that Revere started his historic horse ride that warned, 'the British are coming!'

### Pierce-Hichborn House

Next door is the restored **Pierce-Hichborn House** (open for guided tours only once or twice daily; call Paul Revere House for details), which belonged to Nathaniel Hichborn, Revere's cousin. The asymmetrical,

three-story brick building, built between 1711 and 1715 in the new English Renaissance style, was a radical departure from the Tudor-style wooden dwellings built in the previous century.

## ST STEPHEN'S CHURCH

Exit North Square via Prince Street, following the red bricks of the Freedom Trail back to Hanover Street. Turn right and walk two blocks north to reach **St Stephen's Church ❷**, with its white steeple. Built in 1804 as a Congregationalist Meeting House, this dignified structure is the only one of five Boston churches designed by Charles Bulfinch *(see p.12)* that still stands. In 1813 it became a Unitarian church, and in 1862 it was acquired by the Roman Catholic archbishopric. Eight years later, when Hanover Street had to be widened to accommodate traffic, the church was moved back 12ft (3.7m) and raised 6ft (1.8m); then, in 1965, it was restored to its original level.

## PAUL REVERE MALL

Directly opposite St Stephen's Church is the **Paul Revere Mall**, known locally as the Prado. Built in 1933, this spacious brick courtyard is one of the liveliest public spaces in the North End – a sort of Americanized piazza where kids run around, old folks play cards, and footsore tourists take a breather from the Freedom Trail. In addition to a traditional Italian fountain, the Prado features

**Right:** St Stephen's Church steeple.

a magnificent equestrian statue of Paul Revere, modeled in 1885 by Cyrus Dallin and cast in 1940. On the southern (left) wall, bronze panels recall the history of Boston and its people.

## OLD NORTH CHURCH

At the far end of the Prado a small gate opens to the rear of Christ Church, more popularly known as **Old North Church** ❸ (tel: 617-523-6676; www.oldnorth.com; Mar–May 9am–5pm, June–Oct daily 9am–6pm, Nov–Dec 10am–5pm, Jan–Feb Tue–Sun 10am–4pm; free). Before going into the church, take note on the left of the three-story (originally it was two) brick home of Ebenezer Clough, built in 1712. Next to it is a small garden planted as it would have been in the 18th century, while opposite is a poignant reminder of a more modern event: a Memorial Garden hung with military dog tags for those who have perished in recent wars in Afghanistan and Iraq.

### Interior
Built in 1723, Old North is Boston's oldest church. Its interior, painted white since 1912, sports high pew boxes, designed to keep in the warmth of braziers filled with hot coal or bricks, which were placed on the floor on wintry days. The clock at the rear of the church and the four baroque Belgian cherubs that surround it date back to the opening of the church. So does the organ case, although the actual instrument dates only from 1759. It is still played at the service every Sunday at 11am.

The bust of George Washington, in a niche to the left of the apse, was the first public memorial to the great man, and was said by General Lafayette in 1824 to be 'more like him than any other portrait.' Another historical artefact is the 'third' steeple lantern, lit by President Gerald Ford during the American bicentennial observance at the church in 1975. The church has 37 crypts, containing, it is claimed, 1,100 bodies.

**Above from far left:** Old North Church inside and out.

---

## North End history

On colonial maps the North End looks like an irregular thumb jutting into the Atlantic Ocean, with a canal, called the Mill Stream, cutting it off from the larger Shawmut Peninsula.

By the late colonial period the small cluster of wooden houses had become one of Boston's most fashionable quarters, with several fine brick homes and some of the richest families in town. Unfortunately, many of the prominent residents were Tories who, when the British evacuated in 1776, hightailed it to Canada and took their money with them. Rich Yankees pulled out too, preferring the more genteel atmosphere of Beacon Hill, then being developed. Artisans, sailors, and tradesmen filled the empty houses, and throughout the 19th century the North End was a working man's quarter dominated by the shipping industry.

The Irish poured into the neighborhood in the 1840s, and soon dominated the area politically. Eastern European Jews followed the Irish, and by 1890 had established a thriving residential and business district along Salem Street. The Italians – mostly from Sicily and the southern provinces of the mainland – were the last group to arrive in substantial numbers; by the 1920s they had established an overwhelming majority, and have dominated the neighborhood ever since.

## COPP'S HILL
## BURYING GROUND

Exit from the church, and walk northwest up Hull Street for about 150yds/m to **Copp's Hill Burying Ground** ❹ (daily dawn–dusk), Boston's second-oldest cemetery (after King's Chapel; *see p.27*), where the gravestones, some ornately carved, poke out of the grass like misshapen teeth. Its name comes from that of William Copp, who farmed on the hill's southeast slope in the mid-17th century. In the colonial era, the base of the hill, known pejoratively as New Guinea (after the African country of Guinea), was occupied by the city's first black community, and about 1,000 black citizens are buried in the cemetery's northwest corner.

*Notable tombstones*

In the graveyard's northeast corner a tall black monument commemorates Prince Hall, who helped found Boston's first school for black children, and who was also the founder, in 1784, of the African Grand Lodge of Massachusetts, the world's first black Masonic Lodge. Nearby is the tombstone of 'Capt. Daniel Malcolm, Mercht,' who is remembered for smuggling 60 casks of wine into port without paying the duty. He asked to be buried 'in a Stone Grave 10 feet deep,' secure from desecration. His body may have been safe, but his tombstone was not: on it are scars made by the Redcoats who singled it out for target practice.

## Weekend processions

If you are in Boston in summer, be sure to time your visit to the North End to catch one of the Italian community's local feasts, or *festas*, celebrated in honor of saints' days. They are held almost every weekend in July and August, with Sunday being by far the more exciting day, and usually involve street fairs, brass bands, singers, raffles, food stalls selling sausage and peppers and *zeppole* (fried dough), and processions in which saints' statues are carried, often festooned with contributions of paper money. In the Feast of the Madonna del Soccorso (Our Lady of Succor), celebrated in mid-August, the star of the show is the famous flying angel. Portrayed by a little girl on a pulley, she floats above North Street, her arms outstretched to the crowd, and is lowered to the statue and the procession below. The biggest celebrations are the Fisherman's Feast and St Anthony's Feast in late August.

## Food and Drink 🍴
**④ SORELLE BAKERY AND CAFÉ**
100 City Square, Charlestown; tel: 617-242-5980; www.sorellecafe.com; Mon–Fri 7am–5pm, Sat–Sun 8am–5pm; $
The original is at 1 Monument Avenue, but this branch keeps longer hours and still serves incredible breads and pastries, plus fresh sandwiches and salads.

## CHARLESTOWN

The Freedom Trail's red-brick route leads you along Hull Street to Commercial Street, where you turn left and then right to cross the Charles River on the **Charlestown Bridge ❺**.

Ahead lies the city's oldest settlement, established in 1628, two years ahead of Boston. In 1630 it was the seat of the British government, and on its Breed's Hill the bloody Battle of Bunker Hill was fought on June 17, 1775. The area's prosperity was later tied up with the Navy Yard founded in 1800. At times (usually wartimes), it was the busiest shipbuilding and repair yard in the US, but in 1974 demand slowed to the point where the facility was forced to close – a third of it was taken over by the National Park Service.

Crossing the bridge (don't look down if you suffer from vertigo – the water seems awfully close through the metal grill) provides an excellent view on the left of the **Charlestown Locks**, which control the water level between the river and the Inner Harbor, and, rising majestically in the background, the **Leonard P. Zakim Bunker Hill Bridge** (www.leonardpzakimbunkerhillbridge. org), one of the most striking contemporary structures in the city.

### Paul Revere Park

Below the bridge on the Charlestown side of the river is pretty little **Paul Revere Park ❻**, part of the Harbor-Walk *(see feature, p.75)*. Take the steps down to the park and follow the walkway under the Charlestown Bridge and past the hotel on Tudor Wharf toward the Charlestown Navy Yard.

### City Square

Before exploring the Charlestown Navy Yard, you could take a breather at **Sorelle Bakery and Café**, see ⑪④, facing onto **City Square**, to the northwest. In the square's center a small circle of greenery preserves the foundations of the Great House, dating from 1629 and believed to have been John Winthrop's home and the colony's brief seat of government. The house became the Three Cranes Tavern in 1635, and was destroyed during the Battle of Bunker Hill.

### CHARLESTOWN NAVY YARD

Walk for 100yds/m or so along Constitution Road toward the entrance of **Charlestown Navy Yard ❼**, whose most famous resident is the USS *Constitution (see p.38)*. Just inside the entrance is the **Visitor Center** (tel: 617-242-5601; www.nps.gov/bost; daily Sept–June 9am–5pm, July–Aug 9am–6pm), where you can find out about free tours of the ship and its neighbor, the restored naval destroyer USS *Cassin Young*, which served in the Pacific during World War II. Elsewhere in the National Park Service-administered area you can wander around the old buildings and dry docks used to mend ships. Escape the crowds at the little-visited **Massachusetts Korean War Veterans Memorial**, where you can listen to recordings of veterans remembering the conflict.

**Above from far left:**
Copp's Hill gravestones; clapboard houses in the Bunker Hill neighborhood.

**Narrow house**
Opposite the main entrance to Copp's Hill Burying Ground, take note of the gray-painted clapboard house at 44 Hull Street. At just 9½ft (3m) wide, this is Boston's narrowest home, allegedly built around 1800 by a spiteful man to block the light coming into the neighboring house.

### USS Constitution

Boston-built and first sailed from here in 1797, the **USS Constitution** ❽ (www.ussconstitution.navy.mil; Apr–Oct Tue–Sun, Nov–Mar Thur–Sun 10am–5.30pm; tours on the hour and half-hour) is the world's oldest warship still in commission. It keeps this status thanks to an annual July 4 'turnaround,' when tugs pull it out into the harbor.

On board, Navy enlistees in 1812 uniform conduct guided tours and answer questions. During the busy summer months lines to tour the USS *Constitution* can be long.

Opposite the ship is the **USS *Constitution* Museum** ❾ (tel: 617-426-1812; www.ussconstitutionmuseum.org; daily Apr–Oct 9am–6pm, Nov–Mar 10am–5pm; free, but donations welcome), which simulates the experience of life below decks. You can place your hands on a ship's wheel, climb into a hammock, or hoist the sail on a moving 'deck' while the sounds of shipboard life echo all around. Also on show in the museum is a walk-through model of a keel and ribbing, and a continuous audiovisual program that depicts a bloody sea battle of 1812.

## BUNKER HILL MONUMENT AND MUSEUM

Exit the Navy Yard back onto Constitution Road and turn right to reach Chelsea Street. Duck through the nearby underpass beneath the Tobin Bridge, emerging on Lowney Way. Turn left and then immediately right onto Chestnut Street. Continue along Chestnut Street to the **Bunker Hill Monument** ❿ (www.nps.gov/bost/historyculture/bhm.htm daily 9am–4.30pm; free), a 220ft (67m) high granite obelisk crowning Breed's Hill. The battle was fought just north of the monument.

Climb the 294 stairs to the top for rewarding views of the city. The bronze statue on a pedestal in front of the monument is Colonel William Prescott, the patriot who uttered the immortal line, 'Don't fire until you see the whites of their eyes!' as an instruction to the troops before the battle.

---

## Old Ironsides

During its active service between 1797 and 1855 the USS *Constitution* was a victor in 42 battles. According to legend, it was during an engagement with the British warship *Guerrière* in 1812 that the *Constitution* earned the sobriquet 'Old Ironsides'; on seeing the enemy's cannonballs apparently bouncing off the boat's side, a sailor exclaimed: 'Her sides are made of iron!' The real reason behind the nickname is more mundane: the *Constitution* was constructed of live oak, which is said to be five times more durable than white oak.

On the corner of Monument Square and Monument Avenue is the small **Battle of Bunker Hill Museum** (tel: 617-242-5641; www.nps.gov/bost; daily 9am–5pm; free), where, on the second floor, hangs an excellent reproduction of the *Bunker Hill Cyclorama*, a circular painting that places the viewer at the heart of the battle's action. The original was shown in 1888 at the now demolished Castle Square Theater at 421 Tremont Street in the South End.

## WINTHROP SQUARE

From the southeast corner of Monument Square head downhill along Winthrop Street, which leads into picturesque **Winthrop Square ⑪**. For a century this was a training field where Charlestown boys learned the art of war. At the northwest corner is a gate flanked by bronze tablets commemorating those killed on June 17, 1775.

Return to Winthrop Street and keep going downhill, past the fire station and across Warren Street until you reach the junction with Main Street. Turn right here to find the gourmet pizzeria **Figs**, see ⑪⑤, or a couple of blocks further on the corner of Pleasant Street, the historic **Warren Tavern**, see ⑪⑥, dating from 1780. Both Paul Revere and George Washington once stayed here.

## SAVINGS BANK BUILDING

A few yards north, where Main Street meets Austin Street, stands the handsome Victorian Gothic-style **Savings**

**Bank Building ⑫** at 1 Thompson Square, built in 1875. The interior has been sensitively adapted into offices, a florist, barber, and café, with the bank's enormous vaults still left in tact.

From here a short walk west along Austin Street and across busy Rutherford Avenue will bring you to **Community College Station**, behind Bunker Hill Community College, the end of this route.

Alternatively, amble back through Charlestown, admiring its many old homes, toward the Navy Yard to pick up the Inner Harbor Ferry to Long Wharf *(see box, p.32)*.

Above from far left: Bunker Hill Monument; naval uniform; all aboard the USS *Constitution*.

## Food and Drink 🍴

**⑤ FIGS**
67 Main Street; tel: 617-242-2229; www.toddenglish.com; Mon–Thur 11.30am–10pm, Fri 11.30am–10.30pm, Sat noon–10.30pm, Sun noon–9.30pm; $$
Celebrity chef Todd English's gourmet pizzeria serves the excellent thin-crust pizza grilled in wood-fired ovens and topped with a variety of epicurean toppings. The fig and prosciutto special is a perennial favorite. There's a second location at 24 Charles Street, Beacon Hill, tel: 617-742-3447, good for walk 5 *(see p.50)*.

**⑥ WARREN TAVERN**
2 Pleasant Street; tel: 617-241-8142; www.warrentavern.com; Mon–Fri 11.30am–1am, Sat–Sun 10.30am–1am; $
Named after revolutionary hero General Warren, this historic pub has low ceilings and beams, making it a convivial spot for lunch. Burgers and chunky sandwiches are the specialty. Live music some evenings.

**Below:** historic watering hole.

# HARVARD

*World-famous Harvard University is actually in the separate city of Cambridge, which lies on the north bank of the Charles River. This walking tour takes you around the university's hallowed halls, into some of its excellent museums, and back across the river for fantastic views.*

**DISTANCE** 4 miles (6.5km)
**TIME** A full day including museum visits
**START/END** Harvard Square T Station
**POINTS TO NOTE**
It is difficult to do full justice to all of Harvard's museums in one day. Decide whether you would prefer a brief once-over of everything, or a concentrated session at, say, the natural history museums. Note that the Fogg Art and Busch-Reisinger Museums are closed until 2013 while a new building is being constructed *(see margin, p.43).*

*(see margin, p.43).*

**Below:** 'The Statue of the Three Lies'; Harvard flag; rhino outside Harvard's Biological Laboratories.

### HARVARD YARD

Emerging from **Harvard T Station**, orientate yourself in **Harvard Square ❶**, which is actually an amorphous area rather than a four-sided square. To the west lies the Coop, or Harvard Cooperative Society (a bookstore and department store founded in 1882). To the east **Harvard Yard** has the university's most historic buildings, bordered on the south and west by Massachusetts Avenue. The Yard is the geographic heart of America's oldest

and most prestigious university, founded in 1636. Six of Harvard's graduates have become US President, and it has churned out dozens of Nobel and Pulitzer prize-winners.

Enter Harvard Yard by the Johnston Gate, on the west arm of Massachusetts Avenue. To the right inside the gate is **Massachusetts Hall** (1718); look at its western gable to see the College Clock, painted in 18th-century style. To the left is **Harvard Hall**. This is the third version of the building, dating from 1766; the original, built in 1642, collapsed, and its 1682 replacement was razed by a fire in 1764. The inferno destroyed the largest library in the colonies, including John Harvard's own collection of books.

#### 'The Statue of Three Lies'

Immediately ahead across the grass is **University Hall**, a white granite building designed by Charles Bulfinch in 1814. It now houses university offices, but was originally given over to dining rooms, classrooms, a chapel, and the president's office. The bronze statue of John Harvard in front of University Hall is nicknamed 'The Statue of Three Lies', because it is not of John Harvard, but of an 1884 undergraduate sculpted by Daniel French Chester; the

Above from far left:
Memorial Hall;
students on the steps
of Widener Memorial
Library; colonnade.

inscription refers to John Harvard as founder of Harvard College, when he was in fact only the first major benefactor; and, contrary to the inscription, the college was not founded in 1638, the year of Harvard's bequest, but in 1636.

## NEW YARD

Walk around University Hall into the Tercentenary Quadrangle, or **New Yard ❷**, which, on the first Monday of each June, is the scene of Commencement, Harvard's major graduation ceremony.

New Yard is dominated on the south by the **Widener Memorial Library** (closed to general public), with its grand Corinthian colonnade atop a monumental flight of stairs. Inside lie 56 miles (90km) of shelves, the third-largest library in the country and part of the largest university library in the world (13 million volumes). The Memorial Room, an elegant affair of wood paneling and stained-glass windows, contains Harry Widener's collection of rare books, including a Gutenberg Bible and a First Folio of Shakespeare.

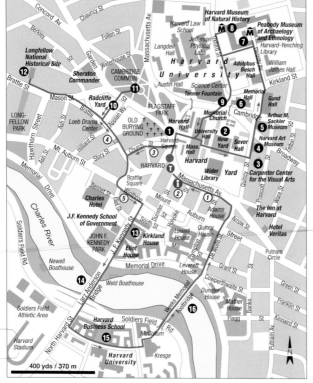

**The swimming test**
The Widener Library is named after Harvard graduate Harry Elkins Widener, who drowned along with his father when the *Titanic* sunk. Legend has it that when his mother donated $2 million to found the library, it was on condition that all Harvard undergraduates pass a 50-yard swimming test. However, the test, no longer administered, predated Harry's attendance at Harvard.

**BEST BURGERS IN AMERICA**, BOSTON GLOBE
**VOTED A 'BOSTON LANDMARK'**, BOS MAGA

**Above from left:**
Eliot House;
Mr Bartley's Burger
Cottage; butterflies in
the Museum of
Natural History;
Peabody Museum.

**Below:** Museum of
Natural History tiger;
campus tour.

### Memorial Church and Sever Hall

The northern side of New Yard is punctuated by the soaring, delicate white spire of **Memorial Church**, which honors the Harvard dead in both world wars.

On the eastern side of the Yard is the Romanesque **Sever Hall**, considered one of architect H.H. Richardson's finest works. Its entrance is flanked by turreted towers, and the entire building is wonderfully rich in decorative brickwork.

## ART MUSEUMS

Walk behind Sever Hall to emerge on Quincy Street, where you will find yourself facing the strikingly modern **Carpenter Center for the Visual Arts** ❸ (tel: 617-495-3251; www.ves.fas. harvard.edu; Mon–Sat 10am–11pm, Sun 1–11pm; free), the only Le Corbusier building in North America. The ground-floor and third-floor galleries host exhibitions by international artists.

### Fogg Art Museum and Busch-Reisinger Museum

Next door at no. 32 are the **Fogg Art Museum** and **Busch-Reisinger Museum** ❹, both currently closed for renovations until 2013 *(see margin, opposite)*. The highlights of the Fogg include works by Ingres, and a fine collection of French Impressionist and Pre-Raphaelite works. In addition, there are dozens of Blake watercolors, and hundreds of Dürer and Rembrandt prints. The Busch-Reisinger collection, specializing in German art, includes 20th-century Expressionist canvases by Klee and Kandinsky, as well as the archives of architects Gropius and Feininger, forming the largest Bauhaus collection outside Germany.

### Arthur M. Sackler Museum

During the renovations, pieces from both collections are being displayed in rotation at the nearby **Arthur M. Sackler Museum** ❺ (485 Broadway; tel: 617-495-9400; www.harvardart museums.org; Tue–Sat 10am–5pm; charge), alongside an outstanding collection of Chinese jades. The Sackler's Ancient and Islamic collections are also noteworthy.

### Lunch options

Either before or after visiting the Sackler, you can backtrack down Quincy Street to Massachusetts Avenue for lunch. Turn right to find **Mr Bartley's Burger Cottage**, see ⑪①, or walk further down the avenue toward Harvard Square and turn left on Holyoke Street to find **Clover**, see ⑪②.

## Harvard tours

For the inside scoop on Harvard, take one of the student-led tours of the campus (Feb–Apr and mid-Sept–mid-Dec Mon–Fri 10am and 2pm, Sat 2pm, mid-June–mid-Aug Mon–Sat 10, 11.15am, 2 and 3.15pm; free), leaving from the Harvard University Information Center, Holyoke Center Arcade (1350 Massachusetts Avenue; tel: 617-495-1573; www.harvard.edu). A fun alternative is the 70-minute Harvard Tour (tel: 617-848-8576; www.harv. unofficialtours.com; Sat–Sun 10.45am, 12.45 and 1.45pm; suggested donation $10), which leaves from Harvard Square outside Harvard T Station.

## MEMORIAL HALL

Return to Quincy Street and follow it north across Cambridge Street. On the left is **Memorial Hall** ❻, a huge, red-brick Victorian Gothic pile, dating from 1874, with polychromatic roofs, which contains the Sanders Theater, the university's largest auditorium. Its somewhat truncated appearance is the result of a fire that destroyed the tall pinnacled roof over the central tower. If the building is open, pop in to admire the stained-glass windows.

On the right of Memorial Hall is the contrasting slender-pillared **Gund Hall**, built in 1969, and home of the Graduate School of Design.

## PEABODY MUSEUM

Cross Kirkland Street and enter Divinity Avenue. This is flanked on the left side by the handsome, medieval-style **Adolphus Busch Hall** (named after the beer baron) and on the other by the William James Hall skyscraper, home to the Behavioral Science Department.

Toward the end of the avenue, on the left at no. 11, is the fascinating **Peabody Museum of Archaelogy and Ethnology** ❼ (tel: 617-496-1027; www.peabody.harvard.edu; daily 9am–5pm; charge). Among its superb collection of artefacts from around the globe are the only surviving Native American objects gathered by the explorers Meriwether Lewis and William Clark, who led the first American overland expedition to the Pacific coast (1804–6), as well as a huge photographic archive.

## MUSEUM OF NATURAL HISTORY

Leaving the Peabody, turn right and right again to follow the footpath around the building to Oxford Street. Here, turn right once more to reach the entrance of the **Harvard Museum of Natural History** ❽ (tel: 617-495-3045; www.hmnh.harvard.edu; daily 9am–5pm; charge). Its most famous exhibit is the collection of over 3,000 extraordinarily lifelike handmade glass flowers. Kids will also love its collection of dinosaur remains, including a 12ft (3.5m) tall Plateosaurus.

## TANNER FOUNTAIN

Exit back onto Oxford Street, and, turning left, continue past the Science Center, the largest building on Harvard campus. In front of it, amid a patch of grass to the north of Harvard Yard, stands the unusual **Tanner Fountain** ❾, gurgling amid a circular

### New art museum

In 2008 the adjoining Fogg Art Museum and Busch-Reisinger Museum closed for major renovations. The plan is to bring the two art museums under the same roof as the Arthur M. Sackler Museum in a new building designed by Renzo Piano, slated to open in late 2013, to be collectively known as the Harvard Art Museum. During the construction period the Sackler's galleries will be reconfigured to show key pieces from the collections of the Fogg and the Busch-Reisinger.

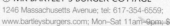

## Food and Drink 🍴

### ① MR BARTLEY'S BURGER COTTAGE

1246 Massachusetts Avenue; tel: 617-354-6559; www.bartleysburgers.com; Mon–Sat 11am–9pm; $
A Harvard institution, this classic mom-and-pop burger joint offers a wide range of burgers named after famous politicians like Bill Clinton and Arnold Schwarzenegger ('this is no girly burger'). Wash them down with a raspberry lime rickey or a thick frappe.

### ② CLOVER

7 Holyoke Street; www.cloverfoodlab.com; daily 7am–10pm; $
They still have their original food truck at MIT (see p.49) but this hip veggie operation, serving local, organic produce, now also has a permanent Harvard base. From granola and yoghurt for breakfast to a chickpea fritter plate for lunch or dinner it's all good.

grouping of 159 boulders – it's a lovely place to rest and take in the passing scene of students during term time.

Re-enter Harvard Yard. After passing Holworthy, Hollis, Stoughton, and Thayer – all freshman dormitories – you will be back by the Johnston Gate.

### RADCLIFFE YARD

Cross Massachusetts Avenue and head west on Church Street. Just off to the left, on Palmer Street, is **Veggie Planet**, see ⑪③. Turn right at the junction with Brattle Street. Continue walking until you pass Appian Way. Next on the right is **Radcliffe Yard** ⑩, which is surrounded by a number of delightful late 19th- and early 20th-century buildings. This is where the

renowned women's college of that name, now fully integrated with Harvard, began life in 1879.

Exit from the yard's far side onto Garden Street, which borders **Cambridge Common** ⑪. Surrounded by a semicircle of cannons, a bronze relief marks the spot where, on July 4, 1775, George Washington assumed command of the Continental Army.

### LONGFELLOW HOUSE

Return through Radcliffe Yard to Brattle Street, and turn right to see why this is Cambridge's most prestigious street. Leafy and tranquil compared to busy Harvard Square, it is lined by splendid clapboard houses fronted by elegant porticoes, most from the 19th century, some from even earlier. Many bear blue plaques commemorating the great names who lived in them.

The most famous is the cream-colored clapboard building at no. 105, where Henry Wadsworth Longfellow composed many of his most famous works. It is now the **Longfellow National Historical Site** ⑫ (tel: 617-876-4491; www.nps.gov/long; June–Oct Wed–Sun, tours 10.30am–3pm; charge). Even if the house *(see feature, right)* is closed, its pleasant grounds are always open for inspection.

Stroll back along Brattle Street toward Harvard Square, perhaps pausing at **L.A. Burdick Chocolate Shop and Café**, see ⑪④, or **The Red House**, see ⑪⑤, across Brattle Square on Winthrop Street.

---

## Food and Drink

**③ VEGGIE PLANET**
Club Passim, 47 Palmer Street; tel: 617-661-1513; www.veggie planet.net; daily 11.30am–10.30pm; $
A vegetarian restaurant with social responsibility. Didi Emmons lives up to her reputation as one of the most inventive vegetarian chefs in the city by creating tasty meatless pizzas and vegan meals. In the evening there's folk music.

**④ L.A. BURDICK CHOCOLATE SHOP AND CAFÉ**
52-D Brattle Street; tel: 617-491-4340; www.burdick chocolate.com; Sun–Thur 8am–9pm, Fri–Sat 8am–10pm; $
A quiet oasis removed from the bustle of Harvard Square. Indulge in delectable handmade chocolates and pastries, accompanied by a great range of teas and coffees. Their hot chocolate is like dessert in a cup.

**⑤ THE RED HOUSE**
98 Winthrop Street; tel: 617-576-0605; www.theredhouse.com; Tue–Sun noon–midnight, Fri–Sat noon–1am; $$
In a quaint red clapboard house, dating from 1802, this charming restaurant with a large outdoor deck serves most of its mains in half-portions – great if you are not so hungry or on a budget.

## TOWARD THE CHARLES RIVER

From Winthrop Street turn right onto John F. Kennedy Street, and walk south past, on the left, the neo-Georgian **Kirkland House ⑬** and **Eliot House**. Each residential co-ed house is a small college with about 400 students, and herein lies much of Harvard's strength: each house has its own administration and a veritable phalanx of tutors; its own library and dining hall; and its own exclusive societies and clubs. The concept was originally that of Edward Harkness, a Yale alumnus who, spurned by his alma mater, donated $13.8 million to Harvard in 1929 for the original seven houses.

On the other side of John F. Kennedy Street, facing Kirkland and Eliot houses, is Harvard's **John F. Kennedy School of Government** (www.hks. harvard.edu), fronted by the riverside John F. Kennedy Park.

Across busy Memorial Drive the handsome **Larz Anderson Bridge ⑭**, named in memory of Nicholas Longworth Anderson, a distinguished colonel in the US Civil War, spans the Charles River. From it there are superb views of the college, and, in the foreground, the Weld Boathouse, home of Harvard's women's crew. The boathouse to the right is home to the men's crew.

## HARVARD BUSINESS SCHOOL

Cross the river, and continue straight on what is now North Harvard Street

for 100yds/m, passing on the right the Harvard playing fields and, on the left, the prestigious **Harvard Business School ⑮**. Turn left and stroll through the campus. Here the neo-Georgian buildings display a consistent rhythm of green doors, white window-frames, and red-brick walls.

Emerging on the school's eastern side, take the footbridge over busy Soldiers Field Road that leads to the **Weeks Memorial Footbridge ⑯**, which again offers an excellent view of some of Harvard's residential buildings.

Cross Memorial Drive and head north along DeWolfe Street aiming for Massachusetts Avenue, where a left turn will bring you back to Harvard Square.

**Above from far left:** graduation day; Weeks Memorial Footbridge; Harvard Business School.

## Longfellow house history

When work started on the house in 1759 it stood amid 116 acres (47 ha) and was one of seven Tory estates occupying the area between Brattle Square and Elmwood Avenue. Abandoned by its owner John Vassal Jr in 1774, when patriots were making life difficult for loyalists in Cambridge, the house served as George Washington's headquarters for nine months during the siege of Boston. Longfellow took up residence as a lodger in 1837, received the house as a wedding gift from his father-in-law, and remained here until 1882.

# CHARLES RIVER AND MIT

*Experience both the relaxed and scientific side of Boston on this loop walk along the banks of the Charles River and through the campus of Massachusetts Institute of Technology (MIT), home to some of the nation's most innovative thinkers and eye-catching architecture.*

---

**DISTANCE** 5½ miles (8.5km)

**TIME** A full day including museum visits

**START/END** Charles/MGH T Station

**POINTS TO NOTE**

If you plan to eat at 'The Trucks' on MIT campus, do this walk on a weekday. An early-morning tour of the Museum of Science is a good idea to avoid the crowds of school-children that can descend on the place later in the day. MIT tours run throughout the year, but a visit during term time is recommended to experience the student atmosphere.

---

**364.4 smoots plus one ear**

That's the length of the Harvard Bridge as measured using Oliver Reed Smoot, MIT class of 1962. For a prank his student buddies used the 5ft 7ins/1.7m Oliver as a yardstick. The paint squiggles counting off smoots along the bridge were retained when it was rebuilt in the 1980s.

Although the fast-moving traffic of Storrow Drive to the south and Memorial Drive to the north seems to isolate the Charles River from the city, pedestrian bridges over these highways mean that this riverside walk is easy to access. The route is popular with joggers, and, if you have a bicycle, it also makes for a very pleasant ride, with a dedicated cycle path most of the way. If you get tired, there are several points where you can exit the walk and hop back on the T.

You may wish to extend the walk along the river to connect with part of the Harvard route *(see p.40)*.

## LONGFELLOW BRIDGE

Exit Charles/MGH T Station on the Beacon Hill (southern) side and walk right toward the pedestrian bridge over Storrow Drive. On the other side turn right and head under the handsome **Longfellow Bridge**, often referred to as the Salt and Pepper Shaker Bridge, after the distinctive shape of its towers.

On the northern side of the bridge you will pass **Teddy Ebersol's Red Sox Fields ❶** (www.redsoxfoundation.org/ebersol), named after a young Red Sox fan who died in a plane crash. Here young athletes train in softball and soccer as well as baseball. Head past the kids' playground and the tennis courts to turn left from Storrow Drive onto the Charles River Dam. A metal grill here crosses the river at its narrowest point.

## MUSEUM OF SCIENCE

Perched on Charles River Dam, with a life-sized model of a T rex outside, is the interactive and educational **Museum**

of Science ❷ (tel: 617-723-2500; www.mos.org; Sat–Thur 9am–5pm, Fri 9am–9pm, July–Labor Day Sat–Thur 9am–7pm; charge), which boasts 600-plus exhibits in six major fields: astronomy, computing, energy, anthropology, industry, and nature.

Also here are the **Charles Hayden Planetarium** (separate charge), offering excellent programs on astronomy, plus laser light shows, and the **Mugar Omni Theater** (separate charge), where IMAX movies are projected onto a giant high-domed screen.

Above from far left: domed Maclaurin Building at MIT; Longfellow Bridge; exhibit at the Museum of Science.

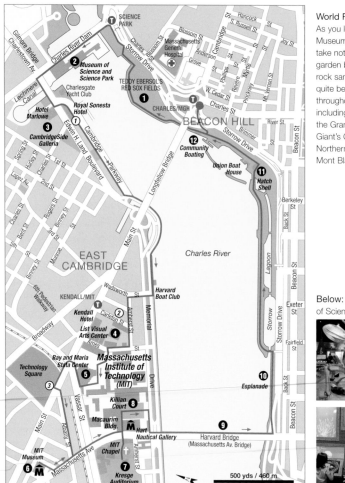

World Rock Garden
As you leave the Museum of Science, take note of the small garden bordered by rock samples, some quite beautiful, from throughout the world, including pieces from the Grand Canyon, Giant's Causeway in Northern Ireland, and Mont Blanc.

**Below:** Museum of Science.

**MIT tours**
Free student-led
tours of MIT's
campus run daily,
at 11am and 3pm,
from the information
center in the lobby of
77 Massachusetts
Avenue (tel: 617-
253-4795).

Boston Duck Tours *(see margin, p.60)* depart from outside the museum.

## EATING OPTIONS

Turn left on leaving the museum and, at the end of the bridge, turn left again onto Edwin H. Land Boulevard, which crosses the narrow Lechmere Canal. To the right is the large shopping mall **CambridgeSide Galleria** ❸ (www. cambridgesidegalleria.com). Alternatively, turn left onto Cambridge Parkway, passing the Charlesgate Yacht Club, to find **Dante**, see ⓄⓄ①, at the back of the Royal Sonesta Hotel.

Continue heading south along the river toward the Longfellow Bridge; the view here of the bridge with the city skyline behind is one of the best on the walk. Pass under the bridge and you will be walking alongside Memorial Drive. Cross this highway just after passing the Harvard Boat Club, walk down Wadsworth Street, and turn left on Amherst Street to enter the MIT campus. On the right at Carleton Street you will find **'The Trucks'**, see ⓄⓄ②.

## MIT

**Massachusetts Institute of Technology** (MIT) was founded in 1861, and has been based here since 1916. Its reputation for science research obscures the fact that there is a fair amount of support for the arts on campus too.

### List Visual Arts Center

Turn right at the end of Amherst Street to arrive at the **List Visual Arts**

**Below:** Simmons Hall dormitory has over 5,500 windows; Kresge Auditorium.

**Center** ❹ (Wiesner Building, 20 Ames Street; tel: 617-253-4680; listart.mit.edu; daily noon– 6pm free), which features temporary exhibits of superb contemporary art.

### Ray and Maria Stata Center

Cross Ames Street and walk toward the whimsical **Ray and Maria Stata Center** ❺ (self-guided tour leaflet available from the information desk), a Frank Gehry building that is is home to MIT's computer science and artificial intelligence lab. Detour over one street west to Main St to find **Area Four**, see ⓄⓄ③, a cool lunch or coffee spot.

### MIT Museum

From Main Street, head south down Albany Stree to Massachusetts Avenue where you should hang a right to reach, at no. 265, the fascinating **MIT Museum** ❻ (tel: 617-253-5927; web.mit.edu/museum; daily 10am– 5pm; charge), which showcases the institute's history, scientific advances, and inventions, as well as the latter's artistic applications; check out the world's largest collection of holographic images. Part of the museum's collection is displayed back on the main campus in the **Hart Nautical Museum** (55 Massachusetts Avenue; same hours; free).

### MIT West Campus

Walk back along Massachusetts Avenue toward the river. Before entering the heart of MIT, through the grand portico on the left, take a moment to look at a couple of buildings on the western side of the campus.

The **Kresge Auditorium** ❼ and the **MIT Chapel** facing it are two buildings designed by a Finnish architect, Eero Saarinen. The auditorium, completed in 1953, is an enormous tent-like structure rising out of a circular brick terrace. Two years later Saarinen designed the tiny multi-faith chapel, which is best appreciated from inside; there are no windows, but light floods in from the ceiling, bouncing off a hanging sculpture by Harry Bertola behind the altar.

### MIT East Campus

From MIT's main entrance walk along the central hallway of the domed Maclaurin Building, known as 'The Infinite Corridor': weather permitting, the sun shines directly into the corridor twice a year. Exit the Maclaurin Building into grassy **Killian Court** ❽ facing the river. At the southern end is a sculpture by Henry Moore (right) and another by Michael Heizer (left).

### HARVARD BRIDGE

Exit from the court and turn right along Memorial Drive. On the left is **Harvard Bridge** ❾ (also known as Massachusetts Avenue Bridge), the longest bridge across the Charles (see margin, p.46), which provides sweeping views both up and down the river. At the bridge's end follow the footpath off to the left to reach the **Esplanade** ❿ (www.esplanadeassociation.org), a riverside park designed by Frederick Law Olmstead. The idyllic Storrow Lagoon, spanned by four small-arched stone bridges, extends for about a mile (nearly 2km).

### BOSTON POPS

Beyond the lagoon is the **Hatch Shell** ⓫ (www.hatchshell.com), where free outdoor concerts, anchored by the Boston Pops Esplanade Orchestra, are held May to September. The highlight is the July 4 concert and fireworks display.

Behind the Shell is the boathouse of the Union Boat Club – the US's oldest rowing club, founded in 1851. Some 300yds/m beyond is the clubhouse of **Community Boating** ⓬ (tel: 617-523-1038; www.community-boating.org), a public sailing program. Next to here is the footbridge back over the highway to Charles/MGH T Station.

Above from far left: Frank Gehry's Stata Center; students by the MIT Chapel; sailboats on the Charles.

Below: near the Hatch Shell is a bust of conductor Arthur Fiedler, who founded the Boston Sinfonietta in 1924, and went on to conduct its successor, the Pops.

## Food and Drink 🍽

### ① DANTE
Royal Sonesta Hotel, 40 Edwin H. Land Boulevard; tel: 617-497-4200; www.restaurantdante.com; Mon–Thur 6.30–10.30am, 11.30am–2.30pm, 5.30–10pm, Fri until 11pm, Sat 7am–2pm, 5.30–11pm, Sun 7am–2pm, 5–9pm; $$$
Dante's outdoor patio, overlooking the Charles River from the back of the Royal Sonesta Hotel, gives it unique appeal. That the three-Michelin-starred chef Dante de Magistris also turns out excellent Mediterranean-inspired cuisine is a bonus.

### ② 'THE TRUCKS'
Carleton Street, MIT Campus; Mon–Fri 11am–3pm; $
Near the Kendall/MIT T Station, these food trucks are an MIT institution. Join throngs of students and alumni working in the area for lunch. Popular ones include Momogoose for light Asian dishes, and Clover (see p.43) for vegetarian options.

### ③ AREA FOUR
500 Technology Square; tel: 617-758-4444; www.areafour.com; bakery/cafe Mon–Fri from 7am, Sat from 9am, restaurant Mon–Wed 11.30am–10pm, Thur–Fri until 11pm, Sat 4pm–11pm; $$
Area Four covers all bases from bakery/café to bar and restaurant. Portions can be small but the ingredients are local and fresh; opt for gourmet pizza, home-made ice creams, and New England ales.

# 5

# BEACON HILL AND THE PUBLIC GARDEN

*Packed with historic buildings, and the location of the Black Heritage Trail, Beacon Hill is one of Boston's most exclusive neighborhoods. A stroll here allows a glimpse into Boston's genteel past and elegant present.*

---

**DISTANCE** 3 miles (5km)

**TIME** A half day

**START** Park Street T Station

**END** Arlington Street T Station

**POINTS TO NOTE**

If you want to tour the State House, do this walk on a weekday. You can easily extend the walk by browsing the many shops along Charles Street.

---

**Below:** ceiling detail from the State House.

The enchanting traffic-free streets of Beacon Hill are a delightful place to explore on foot. The most unswervingly traditional of all Boston's neighborhoods, the Hill has long been associated with wealthy 'Boston Brahmins' – the self-deprecating term coined by Oliver Wendell Holmes for the city's most illustrious families. However, Beacon Hill has always attracted a diverse population, with bohemian types residing on the north or 'bad' side – the derogatory term refers to the social standing of the residents rather than its contrast with the sunnier south side.

## ROBERT GOULD SHAW MEMORIAL

This walk starts at **Park Street Station** at the northeastern corner of Boston Common. Head uphill through the park toward the Massachusetts State House. Immediately opposite this august institution pause to admire the **Shaw-54th Regiment Memorial ❶**, honoring the first regiment of freed blacks in the Civil War. Their leader was 26-year-old white officer Robert Gould Shaw. The relief, sculpted by Augustus Saint Gaudens, depicts the regiment's farewell march down Beacon Street.

## MASSACHUSETTS STATE HOUSE

At the crest of Beacon Street is the **Massachusetts State House** ❷ (tel: 617-727-3676; www.sec.state.ma.us; Mon–Fri 10am–3.30pm; free), designed by Beacon Hill's pre-eminent architect Charles Bulfinch *(see p.12)* and completed in 1798. Dubbed 'the Hub of the Solar System' by Oliver Wendell Holmes, this regal building's most visually impressive feature, the glittering dome crowned in gold leaf in 1861, was originally covered with shingles.

### *Tour of the interior*

Take one of the 45-minute tours here to see the Doric Hall – a vaulted, columned marble hall with a statue of Washington – and the Hall of Flags, which displays the colors of state military units. A double stairway climbs to the chamber of the House of Representatives, an impressive oval room in which hangs the Sacred Cod, a gilded, carved-wood representation of the staple diet of the first settlers in the region and later a mainstay of both Boston's and the state's economy.

## BOSTON ATHENAEUM

A short way further east down Beacon Street is the **Boston Athenaeum** ❸ (tel: 617-227-0270; www.bostonathenaeum. org; Mon–Wed 8.30am–8pm, Thur–Fri 8.30am–5.30pm, Sat 9am–4pm; free), a private library founded in 1807. The building was restored and sensitively extended in 1999; it's well worth signing

up for one of the free tours (Tue and Thur 3pm) otherwise the library hosts art shows that are open to the public. The library's half a million volumes – browsed by the likes of Ralph Waldo Emerson and Nathaniel Hawthorne – are off limits to all but members.

Backtrack to turn right on Bowdoin Street, where you will walk past the side of the State House to reach **Grotto**, see Ⓨ①, a fine lunch option.

## OTIS HOUSE MUSEUM

Before heading into the heart of Beacon Hill, continue down Bowdoin Street until you reach Cambridge Street. A short distance to the left at no. 141 is the **Otis House Museum** ❹ (tel: 617-994-5920; www.historicnewengland. org; Wed–Sun 11am–5pm; charge), the first of three homes in the area that Bulfinch designed in 1796 for Harrison Gray Otis, a real-estate developer turned politician. Today it is owned by the preservation body Historic New England, which has recreated the interior according to how it would have been at the turn of the 19th century.

**Above from far left:**
Beacon Hill facade; Otis House Museum interior; Massachusetts State House.

**Statues at the State House**
Since the State House gardens are off limits to the public, you will have to peer through the front railings to view these statues of famous Bostonians. From left to right they are: the religious martyr Anne Hutchinson, President John F. Kennedy *(pictured)*, educator Horace Mann, Civil War general Joseph Hooker, and another religious martyr, Mary Dyer.

### Food and Drink ⓎⅠ
#### ① GROTTO
37 Bowdoin Street; tel: 617-227-3434; www.grottorestaurant.com; Mon–Fri 11.30am–3pm, 5–10pm, Sat–Sun 5–10pm; $$
The basement location of this boho-chic Italian restaurant might be off-putting on a sunny day, but the food is well worth it. Salads, pastas, and sandwiches are all made with top-grade ingredients.

**Purple glass**
While strolling around Beacon Hill, look out for purple-glass window panes, such as at nos 40 and 39 Beacon Street. A cherished badge of age, the odd color is the result of excess manganese oxide in an early 19th-century shipment of glass from Europe that has darkened after years of exposure to sunlight.

**Below:** snapshots of the Museum of African American History.

## NICHOLS HOUSE MUSEUM

Hike back up Hancock Street, turn right on Derne Street, then at the junction with Joy Street turn left and walk two blocks to Mount Vernon Street to enter the heart of the area. Here the tree-lined streets are narrower and bordered by elegant blocks of red-brick townhouses, enhanced by wrought-iron railings, window boxes of flowers, slender columns flanking doorways, delicate fanlights, and quirky brass door knockers.

Few of these homes are open to the public; one exception is the **Nichols House Museum ❺** (55 Mount Vernon Street; tel: 617-227-6993; www.nicholshousemuseum.org; May–Oct Tue–Sat, Nov–Apr Thur–Sat 11am–4pm; charge), well worth a visit. Inside this 1804 house, attributed to Bulfinch, is preserved the daily life of author and suffragette Ms Rose Standish Nichols, resident from 1885 to 1960.

## PICTURESQUE STREETS

Turn left down Walnut Street, then right onto **Chestnut Street** where nos 13, 15, 17, and 29a provide further examples of Bulfinch's work; the latter is the oldest home on the South slope. Take the first right onto Willow Street and turn immediately left onto cobbled **Acorn Street**, one of Beacon Hill's most picturesque and most photographed streets. Acorn ends in West Cedar Street, where in the 1950s furious residents sat down

on the walkway to save the Hill's brick sidewalks from demolition. A right turn here leads back to Mount Vernon Street.

### Mount Vernon Street

Henry James claimed **Mount Vernon Street** was 'the only respectable street in America.' Glancing up at no. 85, the free-standing **Second Harrison Gray Otis House** (1800), it is difficult to disagree. This Bulfinch building represents his vision of Mount Vernon Street, which he hoped would be lined by mansions, each in its own spacious grounds. Back at no. 88, fronting Louisburg Square, a plaque notes that the poet and Pulitzer Prize-winner Robert Lee Frost lived here from 1938 to 1941 while teaching at Harvard.

### Louisburg Square

No such plaque commemorates Louisa May Alcott, who lived in **Louisburg Square ❻** (the 's' is pronounced) at no. 10. Her literary success with *Little Women* allowed her to move here from the 'bad' side of the hill with her penniless parents and sisters.

The square's dignified red-brick row of houses, among the most expensive in Boston, includes, at the northeast corner, the home of former presidential candidate Senator John Kerry. In the centre is a small iron-fenced residents' park: an undistinguished statue of Columbus stands at the northern end, while at the southern end is one of Aristides the Just, a 5th-century BC Athenian statesman.

*Pinckney Street*

Exiting from the northern side of the square, turn right onto **Pinckney Street**, the dividing line between the posh South Slope and the less desirable North Slope. As well as aspiring writers, such as Louisa May Alcott, who lived at no. 20 with her family before she struck it rich, the street was home in the 19th century to a large and thriving African American community.

The red-brick condominium building at the corner of Anderson Street was once the **Phillips School ❼**, which, when opened to African Americans in 1855, became the city's first interracial school. Across the street at no. 62 is one of several houses that were used as stopovers on the 'Underground Railroad' traveled by fugitive slaves on their way to freedom north of the border in Canada *(see feature, right)*.

At no. 24 is the aptly named **House of Odd Windows**, designed by a nephew of Ralph Waldo Emerson. Across the road, the delightful no. 9½ features an iron gate guarding a tunnel that passes through a house into a hidden courtyard surrounded by three other houses (not open to the public). No. 5-7, the small grey-painted **Middleton-Glapion House**, dates from around 1790, making it one of the Hill's oldest properties.

### MUSEUM OF AFRICAN AMERICAN HISTORY

Turn left onto Joy Street, walk downhill and you will arrive at Smith Court and the **Museum of African Ameri-** can History ❽ (tel: 617-720-2991; www.afroammuseum.org; daily 10am–4pm; charge), housed in the Abiel Smith School, and dedicated in 1834 to the education of the city's African American children. Adjacent is the African Meeting House, the nation's oldest African American church. The museum's displays chart the contribution African Americans made to New England from colonial times through to the 19th century.

*Anti-slavery meetings*

At one time all the houses in Smith Court were occupied by African Americans. Also known as 'Black Faneuil Hall', the African Meeting House hosted anti-slavery meetings that culminated in 1832 with the founding of William Lloyd Garrison's New England Anti-Slavery Society.

Above from far left:
Acorn Street detail; staircase in Nichols House Museum; Louisburg Square.

## Underground Railroad

Beacon Hill was a key stop on the Underground Railroad, an informal network of secret routes and safe houses used by black slaves before the US Civil War to escape the southern US for the northern free states and Canada. Here the runaway slaves found many abolitionists and former slaves who were sympathetic to their cause.

You can find out more about the route while following the Black Heritage Trail. Starting at the Robert Gould Shaw Memorial and running through Beacon Hill, the trail explores the history of Boston's 19th-century African American community. Go to www.afroammuseum.org/trail.htm for a map and a self-guided tour of the trail's 14 sites or contact the National Park Service *(see p.104)* about its daily free guided tours.

## Swanning around

Ever since 1877, taking a turn on the Swan Boats (tel: 617-522-1966; www.swanboats.com; $2.75) on the lagoon of the Public Garden has been a fixture of the Boston scene. The paddle boats, which have been continuously operated by the Paget family, run from mid-April to mid-September, typically from 10am to 4pm.

**Below:** *Make Way for Ducklings* sculpture in the Public Garden; detail from the gates; colorful flowers.

### *Holmes Alley*

Smith Court leads into narrow **Holmes Alley**, one of the 'secret' passageways along which fugitive slaves could escape from their pursuers *(see feature, p.53)* – follow its twists south then west to emerge on South Russell Street.

### VILNA SHUL AND LEWIS HAYDEN HOUSE

At South Russell Street turn left, then right onto Myrtle Street, right again down Irving Street, and left onto Phillips Street. At no. 16 stands the **Vilna Shul** ⑨, (tel: 617-523-2324; www.vilnashul.org; March–end Nov Wed–Fri 11am–5pm, Sun 1pm–5pm;

### 🍴 Food and Drink

**② CAFÉ VANILLE**
70 Charles Street; tel: 617-523-9200; www.cafevanilleboston.com; Mon–Sat 6am–7pm, Sun 7am–7pm; $
Paris-trained bakers Bruno and Philip create mouthwatering cakes and pastries for sale alongside tasty sandwiches and coffee at this cute café, with outdoor tables in summer to enjoy Charles Street's passing parade.

**③ PARAMOUNT CAFÉ**
44 Charles Street; tel: 617-720-1152; www.paramountboston.com; Mon–Thur 7am–4.30pm, 5–10pm, Fri 7am–4.30pm, 5–11pm, Sat 8am–4.30pm, 5–11pm, Sun 8am–4.30pm, 5–10pm; $$
During the day this is an upscale diner with breakfast and lunch options aplenty. At night, it transforms into a candlelit café, with higher prices to match. A branch of the pizzeria Figs *(see p.39)* is a couple of doors down.

free) one of many synagogues that once stood in the area. Now a museum, it dates from 1919 but was founded much earlier in a different location in the now demolished West End. Inside you can find out about how the pews once were part of a Baptist church and how the synagogue inspired Leonard Nimoy to create his Vulcan salute in *Star Trek*.

At no. 66 Philips streets stands **Lewis Hayden House** ⑩, is a private residence that was a famous refuge for runaway slaves. The house was owned by Hayden, a former slave, who threatened to blow up anyone who dared try to search it – no one ever did.

At the end of Philips Street look for Putnam Avenue, a private lane that connects to Charles Street, Beacon Hill's commercial hub.

### CHARLES STREET

Lined with antiques shops, galleries, high-end specialty shops, and eateries, Charles Street is a pleasure to browse. A few hundred yards along on the left, next to **Café Vanille**, see ⑪②, is the former **Charles Street Meeting House** ⑪, now a complex of offices and stores. Recognizable by its lantern tower and clock, it was bought by the African Methodist Episcopalian Church in 1939. Further along, both the **Paramount Café**, see ⑪③, and **Figs** *(see p.39)* are excellent dining options.

### BEACON STREET

Turn left at the junction of Charles and Beacon streets. Facing Boston Common

are some of the grandest Beacon Hill buildings. At **no. 50** ⑫, on the corner of Spruce Street, a plaque commemorates Rev. Blackstone, the original Bostonian, who came to live at this spot – then known as Shawmut by the Native Americans – in 1625.

The Federal-style building at **no. 45** is the third house built by Bulfinch for Harrison Gray Otis, who lived here from 1806 until his death in 1848. It is now occupied by the American Meteorological Society (tel: 617-227-2425; www.ametsoc.org; free), and if you call in advance it is sometimes possible to arrange tours of its interior.

Almost next door, at **no. 42**, the glistening white granite building with two large bow windows belongs to the exclusive Somerset Club. The attitude of this establishment's members can be seen from the time the club caught fire, and firefighters were told to use the tradesmen's entrance – marked by a handsome pair of lion doorhandles.

### THE PUBLIC GARDEN

Retrace your steps back downhill to the corner of Charles and Beacon streets, where you can enter the glorious **Public Garden**, the oldest botanical garden in the US. Although not large, it has magnificently maintained formal flower beds and a lovely lagoon, bordered by weeping willows, on which float the famous Swan Boats *(see margin, left)*.

*Make Way for Ducklings*
Close by the Charles Street entrance is the charming *Make Way for Duck-*

*lings* sculpture ⑬, based on the characters in the classic American children's book of the same name by Robert McCloskey (first published in 1941) – it is always a hit with the little ones.

Head from here toward the miniature suspension bridge over the lagoon. Ahead you will see a splendid equestrian **statue of Washington** ⑭. The first president was also, according to Jefferson, the finest horseman of the age.

Emerge from the garden here at the foot of Commonwealth Avenue where you can start walk 6 *(see p.56)*, or you can continue south to the corner of Arlington and Boylston streets, where you will find the Arlington T stop.

Above from far left: Swan Boats and flowers in the Public Garden.

Below: statue of Washington.

# BACK BAY

*Back Bay, with its neat grid pattern and alphabetical progression of the cross streets from Arlington to Hereford, is bisected by the grand boulevard of Commonwealth Avenue. Around it there are historic mansions and churches, and the choice shopping precincts of Newbury Street and Copley Place.*

**DISTANCE** 3½ miles (5.5km)

**TIME** A half day

**START** Arlington T Station

**END** Symphony T Station

**POINTS TO NOTE**

You may wish to allow time to browse Back Bay's many shops. If you do the walk after lunch, you could end with a sunset drink at the Top of the Hub.

Originally a shallow estuary, Back Bay was filled in and laid out by mid-Victorian believers in the urban grid pattern, eager to make expansive use of 'made land' and put Downtown's tortuous alleys and the narrow streets of Beacon Hill behind them. This was Boston's most exclusive address until the Great Depression of the 1930s saw aristocratic homes converted into apartments and college dormitories. It has now regained its former glory, and is home to Boston's new wealth.

## COMMONWEALTH AVENUE

From Arlington T Station walk north on Arlington Street, passing the brownstone **Arlington Street Church ①** (www.ascboston.org), considered to be the 'mother church' of Unitarianism in the US, and one of first buildings to rise in Back Bay in 1861. Continue past the east end of Newbury Street – there will be a chance to trawl its boutiques later – and the Taj Boston (formerly the Ritz-Carlton and still something of an institution; *see p.111*).

The next corner leads to the foot of **Commonwealth Avenue**, Back Bay's pièce de résistance. Commonly known as Com Ave, this French-inspired boulevard has a 100ft (30m) wide strip

of park adorned by statues running down its middle, the first you'll encounter is of Alexander Hamilton, first Treasury Secretary under President Washington. Magnificent buildings, many once single family homes, line either side of the street. For a glimpse inside one, call in at no. 5, the **Boston Center for Adult Education** (tel: 617-247-3606; www.bcae.org; Mon–Fri 9am–5pm; free). Built in 1904 for Walter C. Baylies, the mansion includes a grand ballroom, reminiscent of the Petit Trianon at Versailles, that the textile industrialist added on for his daughter's coming-out party.

## BEACON STREET

### Gibson House Museum

Turn right on Berkeley Street, walk to the corner of Beacon Street, and turn right again to arrive at no. 137, the **Gibson House Museum ❷** (tel: 617-267-6338; www.thegibsonhouse.org; tours Wed–Sun 1, 2 and 3pm; charge). This 1860 Italian Renaissance-style row house from the first period of Back Bay construction comes complete with original Victorian furnishings, preserved intact through the tenure of the last owner, a scion of the Gibson family who died in the 1950s.

### Isabella Stewart Gardner

Continue west along Beacon Street, where on the right side you will pass **no. 150**. On this spot once stood the home of Isabella Stewart Gardner, Boston's most famous private art collector, before she moved to the Fenway

*(see p.66)*. Mrs Gardner actually lived at no. 152, but when she moved the eccentric heiress insisted that the number never be used again on the street. Her wish has been respected.

### Goethe Institute

A little further along, at no. 170, it is possible to look inside the **Goethe Institute ❸** (tel: 617-262-6050; www.goethe.de/boston; Mon–Fri 9am–3pm; free), a German cultural center based in a 1901 home. On the ground floor is the former ballroom with beautiful moulding decoration, while the library upstairs has a balcony that provides glimpses across the Charles River.

## BACK ON COMMONWEALTH AVENUE

From the Goethe Institute turn left onto Clarendon Street and return to Commonwealth Avenue, where you will note the **First Baptist Church ❹** (www.firstbaptistchurchofboston.org), dating from the early 1870s, and affectionately known as the 'Church of the Holy Bean Blowers' after the trumpeting angels at the corners of its tower. The faces of the frieze (modeled by Auguste Bartholdi, sculptor of the Statue of Liberty) that decorate the top of the church's tower are said to be likenesses of notable Bostonians, such as Longfellow, Emerson, and Hawthorne.

### Notable mansions

Continue down the spine of Commonwealth Avenue to the intersection with Dartmouth Street. The grand corner

**Above from far left:** Boston Public Library and New Old South Church; shoe shop on Newbury Street; Ames-Webster Mansion.

**Firefighters' memorial**
Among the many sculptures dotted along Commonwealth Avenue's central boulevard, one of the most poignant is at the intersection with Clarendon Street – it is the memorial to the nine firemen who died fighting the blaze at the Hotel Vendôme (160 Commonwealth Avenue) in 1973.

**Above from left:**
Trinity Church apse;
Bates Hall reading
room in Boston
Public Library.

**Below:** library lion.

building on the right-hand side is the **Ames-Webster Mansion** ❺ (306 Dartmouth Street), dating from 1872. Much of its elaborate interior design, including a grand hall with carved-oak panels, 18ft (5½m) high ceilings, and stained-glass windows, was preserved when the building was turned into commercial offices later in its life.

Head further down the avenue to the intersection with Hereford Street. On the right is **John F. Andrews House** ❻ (32 Hereford Street), Back

Bay's first Italian Renaissance Revival-style building, now well maintained by an MIT fraternity. On the opposite side, at 314 Commonwealth Avenue, ornamentation runs riot at the flamboyant **Burrage House** ❼, built in 1899, a synthesis of Vanderbilt-style mansion and French chateau.

## SHOPPING ON NEWBURY STREET

Turn left off Commonwealth Avenue at Massachusetts Avenue and walk a block to **Newbury Street**, Back Bay's most eclectic shopping destination. At this end of Newbury the vibe is studenty and hip, as typified by the clientele of **The Other Side Café**, see ⑪①, and **Trident Booksellers and Café**, see ⑪②, next door to which you will find Newbury Comics (www.newburycomics.com), one of Boston's best music, video, and comics stores.

Further down Newbury you can browse antiques stores and art galleries, including, at No. 175, the **Society of Arts & Crafts** ❽ (tel: 617-266-1810; www.societyofcrafts.org; Tue–Sat 10am–6pm), dating back to 1897 and representing over 400 artists from across the US; and at No. 167 **DTR Modern Galleries** (tel: 617-424-9700; www.dtrmodern.com; Mon–Fri 10am–6.30pm, Sat 10am–7pm, Sun noon–6pm) exhibiting pieces from such 20th and 21st century luminaries as Salvidor Dali, Marc Chagall, Damien Hirst and Anish Kapoor.

Newbury Street also has plenty of appealing cafés and restaurants, some

## Food and Drink

① **THE OTHER SIDE CAFÉ**
407 Newbury Street; tel: 617-536-8437; www.theotherside cafe.com; Mon–Thur 11.30am– midnight, Fri 11.30am–1am, Sat 10am–1am, Sun 10am–midnight; $
A hipster hangout with a vegetarian-friendly menu and a nice selection of specialty coffees and beers on tap as well as organic, biodynamic wines. The front patio is a popular place to have drinks or brunch. Movies are screened at 9pm on Sundays.

② **TRIDENT BOOKSELLERS AND CAFÉ**
338 Newbury Street; tel: 617-267-8688; www.tridentbooks cafe.com; daily 8am–midnight; $
The café has expanded and the bookshop shrunk at this convivial place offering simple fare, such as homemade soups, fresh salads, and daily specials. Another plus is their perpetual breakfast.

③ **STEPHANIE'S ON NEWBURY**
190 Newbury Street; tel: 617-236-0990; www.stephanieson newbury.com; Mon–Sat 11.30am–11pm, Sun 10am–10pm; $$
Stephanie's large outdoor patio is the place to see and be seen while dining on Newbury Street. The salads are the stars, but the rest of the menu is tasty too. In chillier weather enjoy a drink by the side of the roaring fireplace.

④ **PARISH CAFÉ**
361 Boylston Street; tel: 617-247-4777; www.parishcafe.com; Mon–Sat 11.30am–1am, Sun noon–1am; $$
The menu of sandwiches designed by some of Boston's celebrity chefs is a little gimmicky but it nevertheless works. There is an extensive list of beers and other drinks, and the outdoor patio in the summer complements the experience.

with street-side dining in the warmer months; a classic option is **Stephanie's on Newbury**, see ⑪③. The closer you get to Arlington Street the more upmarket the stores become, featuring the likes of Giorgio Armani, Brookes Brothers, and the jewelers Shreve, Crump & Low at No. 39.

## COPLEY SQUARE

Turn right at the junction with Arlington, then left onto Boylston Street, where you will hit Arlington T Station, a possible exit point from this walk if you are feeling tired, and the **Parish Café**, see ⑪④, if you fancy lunch. Back Bay still has plenty more to offer, so, if you wish to continue, head straight down Boylston three blocks to reach **Copley Square ❾**, named after the great Boston painter John Singleton Copley and one of the city's focal points.

### Trinity Church

Copley Square's most renowned building, on the eastern side, is **Trinity Church** (tel: 617-536-0944; www.trinitychurchboston.org; Mon, Fri–Sat 9am– 5pm, Tue and Thur 9am–6pm, Sun 1–6pm; charge), a seminal work in American architecture that initiated the Romanesque revival. Enter through the west porch, which leads into a richly decorated interior. The superb frescoes are the work of John La Farge, who also supervised the stained-glass windows.

Rising up 62 stories behind the church is the I.M. Pei-designed **John Hancock Tower**, with 10,000 panels of mirrored glass reflecting all around it.

### Boston Public Library

Facing the western side of Copley Square is the venerable **Boston Public Library ❿** (tel: 617-536-5400; www.bpl.org; Mon–Thur 9am–9pm, Fri–Sat 9am–5pm, Sun 1–5pm; free), designed by Charles Follen McKim in 1852. The interior of the old wing is spectacular. Climb a grand stairway to the second floor to view one of the library's murals, a painting of the Nine Muses by the Parisian artist Puvis de Chavannes.

On the right is **Bates Hall**, an enormous reading room with a barrel-vaulted ceiling, named after Joshua Bates, the library's first major benefactor. An adjoining room displays Pre-Raphaelite murals.

Go up one more floor to see the **John Singer Sargent Gallery**, featuring a series of murals on religious themes.

**Library tours**
There are often fine-art and photography exhibitions in the Boston Public Library. Free art and architecture tours depart from Dartmouth Street lobby in the old wing (Mon 2.30pm, Tue 6pm, Fri and Sat 11am).

**Below:** Trinity Church and John Hancock Tower.

The lovely Italian-cloistered **courtyard** in the center of the building is one of the city's most peaceful retreats, and you can enjoy it with refreshments from **The Courtyard**, see ⑪⑤.

### New Old South Church

Opposite the Public Library on the corner of Bolyston and Dartmouth streets is the striking Italian Gothic campanile of the **New Old South Church** ⑪ (www.oldsouth.org), dating from 1875. The original Old South still stands Downtown; visit on walk 1 *(see p.29)*. The church's original 246ft (75m) tower, which began to lean soon after construction, had to be dismantled and rebuilt slightly lower in 1931.

**Duck Tours**
Departing from
Huntington Avenue,
between Copley
Place and the
Prudential Center, are
the popular Duck
Tours (tel: 617-267-
3825; www.boston
ducktours.com; Apr–
Nov 9am–dusk; $26),
which use amphibious
vehicles built in World
War II (nicknamed
'ducks') for the 90-
minute narrated land
and water circuit
around Boston. The
same tour can also
be joined outside the
Museum of Science
(see pp.46–7);
advance booking
is advised.

### COPLEY PLACE

Head in the other direction toward where Huntington Avenue meets Darmouth Street at the entrance to the Westin Hotel, which is part of **Copley Place** ⑫, central Boston's largest and glitziest shopping and office complex. Follow the corridors through the building to arrive at two floors of upmarket stores surrounding a nine-story atrium, in the center of which is a 60ft (18m) travertine and granite waterfall sculpture.

### PRUDENTIAL CENTER

An enclosed walkway from Copley Mall leads you over Huntington Avenue into the **Prudential Center**, another shopping mall surrounding the 52-story Prudential Tower. On the 50th floor is the **Skywalk** ⑬ (tel: 617-859-0648; www.topofthehub.net; daily Apr–Nov 10am–10pm, Dec–Mar 10am–8pm; charge), which provides 360-degree views of the city through floor-to-ceiling windows, as well as the *Dreams of Freedom* exhibition about the history of immigration in Boston. This is an ideal spot to return to at the end of the walk to enjoy a cock-tail at the **Top of the Hub**, see ⑪⑥, the restaurant and bar on the tower's 52nd floor.

Unless you hire a helicopter to fly over the city, the bird's-eye views from either of Prudential's venues are pretty excep-tional; the viewing gallery at the top of the nearby John Hancock Tower, for example, closed after 9/11.

## CHRISTIAN SCIENCE PLAZA

Exit the Prudential Center at the corner of Huntington Avenue and Belvidere Street, across from which lies the 670ft (200m) long reflecting pool that forms the centerpiece of the **Christian Science Plaza ⓮**, designed by I.M. Pei in the early 1970s and one of the most monumental public spaces in the city.

### Christian Science Church

Along the north side of pool runs the five-story Colonnade Building, culminating in the separate **Christian Science Church ⓯** (tel: 617-755-3345; christianscience.com; Tue noon–4pm, Wed 1–4pm, Thur–Sat noon–5pm, Sun 11am–3pm; free), the original church of the movement founded by Mary Baker Eddy (1821–1910) and headquartered in Boston since 1882.

The church is entered through a dramatic basilica-like structure, a mixture of Byzantine and Italian Renaissance styles. As you will discover on the guided tour, this part is the church's 1906 extension that seats 3,000 on three levels. The pipe organ here is one of the largest in the Western hemisphere.

Tucked behind this is the original Mother Church from 1894, with 82 beautiful stained-glass windows depicting biblical events.

### Mary Baker Eddy Library and Mapparium

On leaving the church, immediately to the right, with its entrance at 200 Massachusetts Avenue, is the **Mary Baker Eddy Library and Mapparium ⓰** (tel: 617-450-7000; www.marybakereddylibrary.org; Tue–Sun 10am–4pm; charge). The highlight of the beautifully designed interior is the Mapparium (last show at 3.40pm), a globe 30ft (9m) in diameter, made up of 608 stained-glass panels, and into which you can walk. It provides a snapshot of the world as it was in 1935. The echoing acoustics are uncanny.

Exit from the library onto Massachusetts Avenue. Head southeast along the road and you will eventually come to Symphony T Station.

**Below:** Christian Science Church.

# BACK BAY FENS

*Beyond Massachusetts Avenue, architecturally dense Back Bay yields to the Fenway, a loose scattering of institutions and apartment buildings joined by the meandering path of the Back Bay Fens, an urban archipelago of parkland.*

**Red Sox tickets**
The Red Sox are so popular that tickets for a game are snapped up as swiftly as they go on sale. Check the Red Sox website for what's available, or turn up early (real early) on match day for standing-room-only tickets, sold from the Gate C ticket window.

**DISTANCE** 1¼ miles (2km)
**TIME** 2 hours
**START** Kenmore T Station
**END** Longwood Medical Area T Station
**POINTS TO NOTE**
This walk can be combined with tour 8 covering the Museum of Fine Arts and the Isabella Stewart Gardner Museum. The area around Victory Gardens in the Fens is a notorious gay cruising area and site of muggings, so bear in mind that it is not safe to explore at night.

## Food and Drink

**① UBURGER**
636 Beacon Street; tel: 617-536-0448; uburgerboston.com/boston; Mon–Sat 11am–11pm, Sun noon–11pm; $
This generic-looking café is feted by Boston burger-lovers. They grind their own prime beef, hand-cut their fries and onion rings, and charge from $4.50 for their burgers. At lunch the line can be out the door.

**② LA VERDAD TAQUERIA**
1 Lansdowne Street; tel: 617-421-9595/617-351-2580; www.laverdadtaqueria.com; counter: Tue–Thur 11am–1am, Fri–Sat 11am–2am; restaurant: Tue–Thur 5pm–1am, Fri 5pm–2am, Sat 11am–2am; $–$$
At the end of Boston's main nightclub strip, chef Ken Oringer's latest venture, specializing in Mexican street food, is a sharp departure from his gourmet restaurant Clio (*see p.111*). Tortillas are made on premises and sauces from scratch. The *carne asada* soft tortilla is excellent.

### KENMORE SQUARE

Begin at **Kenmore Square ❶**, where Commonwealth Avenue, Brookline Avenue, and Beacon Street meet beneath the gaze of the giant Citgo sign. If you arrive by the T, take the Fenway exit to emerge on the southern side of Commonwealth Avenue. On the northern side of the Square you will find **Uburger**, see ⊕①, and further west along Commonwealth Avenue lies the sprawling campus of Boston University.

### FENWAY PARK

Hang a left into Brookline Avenue and head over the Massachusetts Turnpike for a view of the back of the Green Monster. This is the nickname of the left field wall of **Fenway Park ❷** (tel: 617-226-6666; www.redsox.com; tours non-game days: 9am–4pm, game days 3½ hours prior to game time; charge), home to the Red Sox baseball team.

Built in 1912, Fenway Park is the smallest and oldest stadium in the major leagues. Baseball legends like Ted Williams and Carl Yastrzemski played their entire careers here. Red Sox fans, heartbroken since 1918, the last year Boston won a World Series, rejoiced when the team brought home the trophy in 2004 and again in 2007. Tours

of the ground allow you to peer into the press box and down from the Monster.

Walking around the ground's perimeter, turn left into Yawkey Way where you will find the official store for Red Sox souvenirs. Turn left at Van Ness Street and walk along the ball park's southern side to encounter a statue of **Ted Williams ❸** beside Gate B. You could continue down Ipswich Street to grab a snack at **La Verdad Taqueria**, see ⑪②. Turning right from Ted's statue will quickly bring you to Bolyston Street across which are the Back Bay Fens.

## BACK BAY FENS

The reedy marshland along the Muddy River (a creek, actually) is a major link in the Emerald Necklace – nine green spaces designed by Frederick Law Olmsted, also responsible for New York's Central Park. Immediately across Park Drive from Boylston Street are the **Fenway Victory Gardens ❹** (www.fenwayvictorygardens.com; free), a 7-acre (3 hectare) allotment site created in 1942. There are charmingly crafted small gardens here with flower beds, rockeries, and pergolas. Further around the Fens, just south from Agassiz Road, is the more formal **James P. Kelleher Rose Garden ❺**, established in 1930.

## ART SCHOOLS

A footbridge at the southern end of the Fens will take you across the creek to the Fenway entrance of the **Museum of Fine Arts** *(see p.64)*. Next to it, on the corner of Museum Road and Evans Way, is the **School of the Museum of Fine Arts ❻** (tel: 617-267-6100; www.smfa.edu; free), which hosts exhibitions by students and up-and-coming artists. Outside stands Katherine Lane Weerns' regal bronze statue *Rhinoceros*.

More contemporary art can be seen in the galleries of nearby **Massart ❼** (621 Huntington Avenue; tel: 617-879-7000; www.massart.edu; free), the Massachusetts College of Art, just southwest across Evans Way. Hop back on the T at Longwood Medical Area Station.

Above from far left: the Citgo Sign, an unlikely emblem of Boston, has lorded it over Kenmore Square since 1965; baseball at Fenway Park; Red Sox fan.

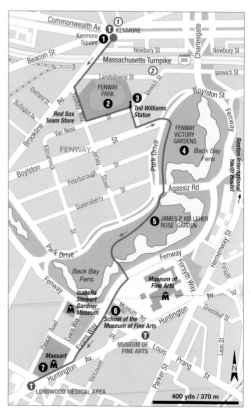

# 8

# TWO ART MUSEUMS

*Hard on the heels of a new wing and renovations at the Museum of Fine Arts comes a Renzo Piano-designed addition to the Isabella Stewart Gardner Museum. Exploring the wonderful collections of these two storied museums will take you from Egyptian antiquities to ambitious 21st-century works.*

**Museum events**
From Wednesday to Friday, there is a highbrow selection of world cinema screened in the MFA's Remis Auditorium, while live music is held in the Calderwood Courtyard in summer (see www.mfa.org). The Calderwood Performance Hall in the new wing of the Isabella Stewart Gardner Museum hosts a variety of music performances, typically on Sunday afternoons and Thursday evenings (see www.gardnermuseum.org)

**DISTANCE** ¼ mile (0.5km)
**TIME** A full day
**START/END** Museum of Fine Arts T Station
**POINTS TO NOTE**
The distance above covers the short walk between the two museums. An evening visit to the MFA is possible Wednesday to Friday, while the Gardner is open until 9pm every Thursday.

Such are the treasures contained inside these two museums that you should set aside a day for them – to spend anything less would be doing the wonderful collections a disservice. The Museum of Fine Arts T stop makes getting here and away a breeze, although if you are quick getting around the museums, you can easily add on walk 7 *(see p.62)* to stretch your legs further across the Back Bay Fens. The hardest decision all day is likely to be choosing in which of the institutions' excellent cafés to have lunch.

## MUSEUM OF FINE ARTS

Second only to New York's Metropolitan among American museums, the **Museum of Fine Arts ❶** (MFA; 465 Huntington Avenue; tel: 617-267-9300; www.mfa.org; Sat–Tue 10am–4.45pm, Wed–Fri 10am–9.45pm; charge) first opened in 1870. It moved into the present building, designed by Guy Lowell, in 1909. The I. M. Pei Wing was added in 1981 and the Foster + Partners-designed Art of Americas Wing opened in November 2010.

The highly cultured citizens of 19th-century Boston were keen collectors, amassing art and antiquities from around the world. Their bequests have resulted in the MFA not only having one of the foremost holdings outside Paris of Impressionist painting (in particular works by Monet, Pissarro, Sisley, Renoir, and Manet), but also an outstanding collection of Japanese and other Asian art. The American art collection is also one of the best in the US and those of Nubian and Egyptian

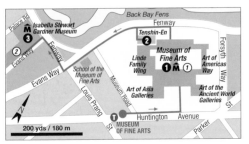

artefacts are practically unrivaled too. Decorative arts include superb displays of silver, porcelain, furniture, jewellery, and musical instruments.

*Planning your visit*

There is so much to see here that time-pressed visitors are well advised either to pick out just one or two collections, or take one of the (free) guided tours that highlight curators' favourite pieces from all the collections.

Approach the MFA from the T Station, and enter at the Huntington Street entrance, outside of which Cyrus Edwin Dallin's bronze equestrian statue *Appeal to the Great Spirit* has stood since 1913.

*Art of the Americas Wing*

The MFA's excellent collection of American art is housed in the new four-level Art of the Americas Wing.

Among the works to look out for are portraits by John Singleton Copley, Gilbert Stuart (including the one of George Washington that was the source of the design on the dollar bill), and John Singer Sargent: his *The Daughters of Edward Darley Boit* is a particularly striking composition, and he painted the spectacular murals of scenes from Greek mythology around the **Upper Rotunda** in the centre of the MFA.

Other highlights include paintings from the mid-19th century Hudson River School and those of Edward Hopper from the 20th century. There is also a fine collection of American decorative arts, including silver made by Paul Revere.

In the glass-enclosed courtyard linking the new to the old building is the **New American Café** see ⑪①, an ideal place to refuel before tackling the rest of the museum.

**Above from far left:** the Museum of Fine Arts and Cyrus Edwin Dallin's sculpture *Appeal to the Great Spirit*; the gallery of Renaissance art.

**Below left:** Renoir's *Dance at Bougival* (1883).

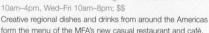

## Food and Drink

### ① NEW AMERICAN CAFE

Museum of Fine Arts, 465 Huntington Avenue; Sat–Tue 10am–4pm, Wed–Fri 10am–8pm; $$

Creative regional dishes and drinks from around the Americas form the menu of the MFA's new casual restaurant and café. There's a three course tasting menu ($29) or you can enjoy tasty gourmet sandwiches and burgers, such as the corn-dusted clam po'boy ($18).

### ② GARDNER CAFÉ

Isabella Stewart Gardner Museum, 280 Fenway; tel: 617-566-1088; Tue–Fri 11.30am–4pm, Sat–Sun 11am–4pm; $$

This well-regarded café has found a expanded home in the Renzo Piano addition to the museum; in good weather there is outdoor seating. The seasonal menu is delicious enough to throw local reviewers into fits of ecstasy, particularly over its famous bread pudding. You can eat here without paying to visit the museum.

### MFA dining

Apart from its New American Café (see p.65), the MFA also offers a fine dining restaurant, Bravo (tel: 617-369-3474; daily 11.30am–3pm, Wed–Fri 5.30–8.30pm). For more casual drinks and snacks there's the café and wine bar Taste (Mon, Tue, Sat and Sun 11.30am–4pm, Wed–Fri 11.30am–8pm) on the first floor of the Linde Family Wing for Contemporary Art and the self-service Garden Cafeteria (10.30am–4pm), with seating in summer out in the Calderwood Courtyard.

### Asian art

Visitors to the MFA are frequently surprised to find it has one of the largest collection of Japanese art outside Japan, spread over two floors of **the Art of Asia, Oceania and Africa** in the museum's southwestern section. A highlight is a temple-like room displaying six massive Buddhas. Take time also to view the intricate beauty of the displayed woodblock prints, textiles, and painted silk screens.

### Contemporary art

Another recent transformation at the MFA has been the unveiling of the Linde Family Wing for Contemporary Art, located in the I. M. Pei designed portion of the museum. This wing's seven thematically-installed collections aim to make contemporary art more accessible to visitors, jolting them with provoking questions and quirky new ideas and designs. Neon, video, sound and metallic tapestry are all part of the fascinating mix.

### Egyptian treasures

For 40 years from 1905, Harvard University and the MFA collaborated on an archeological excavation in Egypt, based at the Great Pyramids at Giza. From this the museum acquired a world-famous collection of **Egyptian antiquities**, located in the Art of the Ancient World galleries. Among many Old Kingdom sculptures is a beautiful statue of King Mycerinus, who built the Third Pyramid at Giza, and his queen, dated to around 2548–2530BC. Other treasures include gilded and painted mummy masks, and some remarkably well-preserved hieroglyphic inscriptions.

The Giza expedition's director, Dr George A. Reisner, also worked in the Sudan, and brought home a dazzling collection of Nubian artifacts, the best in the world outside Khartoum. Particularly awe-inspiring are the exquisite gold jewelry, inlaid with enamel and precious stones, and sculptures, varying in size from huge statues of Nubian kings to tiny funerary figurines.

### Tenshin-En

Exit the MFA via its State Street Corporation Fenway Entrance flanked by *Night & Day*, two giant bronze baby heads by Antonio López García. Before moving on the next museum, gather your thoughts in the MFA's Japanese-style walled garden, **Tenshin-En ❷** (mid-April to mid-October, 10am to

### Renzo's vision

Much of the charm of the Isabella Stewart Gardner Museum is the result of a stipulation in Mrs Gardner's will that everything in the palazzo remain exactly as she arranged it. However, over a century into the museum's life, with annual admission numbers of over 200,000, it was becoming clear the building was straining at its seams. Award-winning Italian architect Renzo Piano was hired to design a new wing, creating a more fitting entrance to the museum, and to house such things as the café, greenhouses, education centre, and other visitor services. The museum's famous musical events also have a new home here in a 300-seat performance hall with three balcony levels surrounding a central stage. The mainly glass structure allows views of Fenway Court and is an inspired, modern complement to Gardner's unique creation.

4pm). Meaning the Garden of the Heart of Heaven, this tranquil space was designed by Kyoto artist Kinsaku Nakane to suggest the landscape of New England.

## ISABELLA STEWART GARDNER MUSEUM

Follow the Fenway around to Evans Way Park and the new entrance *(see feature, opposite)* to the magical **Isabella Stewart Gardner Museum** ❸ (tel: 617-566-1401; www.gardnermuseum. org; Tue–Sun 11am–4.20pm; charge). Fenway Court, the Venetian-style palazzo that houses the museum, was built in 1902 by heiress Isabella Stewart (1840–1924), an eccentric New Yorker who married Jack Lowell Gardner. She scandalized Boston society by drinking beer rather than tea, and walking her pet lions in the Back Bay. Her portrait by John Singer Sargent reveals what was then considered a daring décolletage, but on seeing the notorious picture here at Fenway Court (it hangs in the Gothic Room on the third floor), you might well wonder what all the fuss was about.

### The collection

The renowned art historian Bernard Berenson advised Mrs Gardner on acquisitions, but their presentation and positioning is the result of her inimitable approach.

Among the eclectic collection you will see Dutch baroque and Italian Renaissance masterpieces, Titians and Rembrandts, Whistlers and Sargents, Matisses and Manets, stained glass, and textiles. As part of the museum's renovation, the Tapestry Room, which used to double up as a concert venue, has been restored to its original glory.

Even those impervious to the aesthetic qualities of this impressive collection are sure to delight in the central courtyard and museum's gardens. As well as an art collector, Mrs Gardner was also a passionate horticulturalist and gardner. Many of the courtyard's elements were imported from Venice, and it is ablaze with flowers and greenery throughout the year. To sit here, far from the madding crowd, is sheer bliss.

For refreshments head to the **Gardner Café**, see ⑪② *p.65*, in the new wing.

**Above from far left:** Japanese-style garden Tenshin-En; Upper Rotunda; the MFA features an impressive collection of Egyptian treasures; courtyard of the Isabella Stewart Gardner Museum.

**Left:** John Singer Sargeant's 'daring' portrait of Isabella Stewart Gardner.

# THE SOUTH END

*Few Boston neighborhoods have gone on such a roller-coaster ride of respectability and real-estate values as the South End. Today it is a magnet for artists, trendy singletons, and young families, all attracted by the area's architecture, shops, galleries, and restaurants.*

---

**DISTANCE** 2¾ miles (4.5km)

**TIME** A half day

**START/END** Back Bay/South End T Station

**POINTS TO NOTE**

Do this walk in the morning, so you can have breakfast at Charlie's Sandwich Shoppe. You may wish to extend the time taken to walk the route by browsing the South End's many shops and galleries.

---

The South End, immediately south of Back Bay, is delineated by the Southwest Corridor, Berkeley Street, and Harrison and Massachusetts avenues. A protected historic district, little has changed since it was laid out in the mid-19th century, making the South End a delightful area to explore.

An impressive ethnic diversity characterizes much of the neighborhood,

**Below:** Charlie's Sandwich Shoppe.

with scores of nationalities residing here. It is inner-city Boston's most recognizably gay area, although these days preppy young heterosexual families are more common on its streets.

## CARLETON COURT PARK

Start this route at the Dartmouth Street exit of **Back Bay/South End Station**, beside Copley Place Mall. Taking up much of Carleton Street is **Carleton Court Park ❶**, which is part of the Southwest Corridor, a 52-acre (21-hectare) landscaped ribbon of park that runs for several miles southwest toward the suburb of Jamaica Plain.

## BRADDOCK PARK

Walk through the park and exit left onto **Braddock Park ❷**. This small street is typical of the leafy residential squares that pepper the South End, all of which have a long, narrow garden, enclosed by wrought-iron railings. The terrace houses that line the sides of the street are entered by steep stoops which often rise a full story to the second floor.

At the end of Braddock Park, you could turn left on Columbus Avenue to enjoy a fine breakfast at **Charlie's Sandwich Shoppe**, see 🍴①.

---

## Food and Drink 🍴

**① CHARLIE'S SANDWICH SHOPPE**

429 Columbus Avenue; tel: 617-536-7669; Mon–Fri 6am–2.30pm, Sat 7.30am–1pm; $

The 'best breakfast in America' is promised at this touchstone of the South End, and they are not kidding. Enjoy their delicious turkey hash and poached eggs and the priceless atmosphere of a traditional diner, with hospitable staff and regular patrons to match.

## HARRIET TUBMAN PARK

Cross Columbus Avenue to reach its sharp-angled intersection with Warren Avenue. Here you will find tiny **Harriet Tubman Park ❸**, standing in the lee of the Concord Baptist Church, and graced with two impressive statues. The park is dedicated to the 'Moses of the South,' a runaway slave who organized the 'Underground Railroad,' a network of abolitionists who helped thousands of slaves escape to freedom *(see feature, p.53)*. The red-brick church was built in the 1870s, when many Baptist congregations moved to the South End.

## JORGE HERNÁNDEZ CULTURAL CENTER

From the park follow tranquil Pembroke Street south to Tremont Street. Turn right and cross the road to find West Newton Street. At no. 85 the **Jorge Hernández Cultural Center ❹** (tel: 617-927-1737; www.iba-etc.org/claboston/JHCC_Rental.html) is housed in a converted 19th-century church. The center provides an arts space for the South End's large Hispanic community. On its exterior is a colourful mural and next door there is a kid's playground.

Return to Tremont Street and continue west toward the major junction

**Above from far left:** South End bar; neighborhood skyline; musician in the Jorge Hernández Cultural Center.

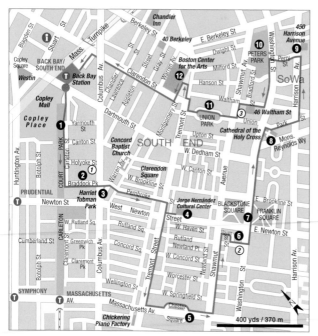

**Naming Boston**
Running parallel to the Carleton Court Park is St Botolph Street, named after the monk for whom England's Boston – and also this city – was named.

**Above from left:**
contemporary theater at the Boston Center for the Arts; cupcakes at Flour Bakery.

**SoWa events**
The first Friday of the month, between 5 and 9pm, members of the SoWa Artist Guild open up their studios. In May they also organize the weekend SoWa Art Walk (sowaartwalk.com). South End Open Studios (www.usea boston.com) takes place on a Sunday in September, while every Sunday from mid-May to mid-October a farmers' and crafts market is held in the car park next to 530 Harrison Avenue (www.sowao penmarket.com).

with Massachusetts Avenue. Across the intersection you won't miss the octagonal tower of the old **Chickering Piano Factory**, built in 1850. It was converted into artists' studios and apartments in 1974.

### CHESTER SQUARE

Turn left from Tremont Street onto Massachusetts Avenue and walk south-west into **Chester Square** ❺, planned in 1850 as an oval park and once the grandest of the South End's squares. Try to imagine how the square looked then, with a fountain at the center rather than the six lanes of traffic that bisect it now.

Ducking left into the far more pleasant Shawmut Avenue, continue until you reach narrow **Haven Street** ❻, where you should hang a right to discover, at **no. 9**, a charming wooden house (*c.*1830) that is one of only two such remaining in the South End.

Facing the house are the Rutland Washington Community Gardens, small allotments of which there are several in the area. You can pause for refreshments at **Flour Bakery and Café**, see ⑪②, on the corner of Rutland and Washington streets.

### BLACKSTONE AND FRANKLIN SQUARES

A block northeast of the Flour Bakery, grassy **Blackstone and Franklin squares** ❼ lie either side of Washington Street. Planned by Charles Bulfinch as a whole oval square in 1801, it was eventually constructed in 1847 as two separate, identical spaces. The cast-iron centerpiece fountains are original. The elaborate edifice that graces Franklin Square at 11 East Newton Street was formerly the St James, one of the city's most elegant hotels. It now serves as apartments.

### CATHEDRAL OF THE HOLY CROSS

Further northeast along Washington Street, at no. 1400, it is impossible to miss the towering granite facade of the **Cathedral of the Holy Cross** ❽ (tel: 617-542-5682; holycrossboston. com; free). Finished in 1875, and still one of the world's largest Gothic cathedrals, it is the seat of the Catholic archbishop in Boston. Pop inside to view the enormous interior, with seating room for 3,500, and many stained-glass windows.

---

## South End history

The marshlands of the South End started to be filled in for construction in the 1830s. By the 1870s the area was fully developed into a grid of red-brick stooped row houses, often laid out, English-style, around squares and small parks.

For a brief period the South End was the place to live, but by the end of 19th century its wealthier residents had decamped to the more fashionable Back Bay, leaving the area largely to the working class and poor immigrants. Many private homes turned into rooming houses. The area's downward spiral continued well into the 20th century; only in the early 1970s did the South End begin to appeal to 'urban pioneers', who saw the intrinsic value of the run-down buildings and were willing to restore them.

## SOWA

Turn right beside the cathedral into Union Park Street, continuing to the junction with Harrison Avenue where you should turn left. You are now in the heart of hip **SoWa** (South of Washington), where warehouses have been converted to galleries, studios, loft-style apartments, restaurants, and shops.

SoWa's focal point is **no. 450 Harrison Avenue ❾** www.sowaartistsguild.com), which hosts 50-plus artists' studios and exhibition spaces. There are several other galleries around here too, including one in the art-lover's bookstore **Art Libris** (500 Harrison Avenue), which specializes in out-of-print art books.

## PETERS PARKS

From Harrison Avenue follow little Perry Street northwest back to Washington Street. Dead ahead is recently relandscaped **Peters Park ❿**, with its striking Soul Revival mural.

Turn left and then, after the park, right into Waltham Street. At **no. 46** is another collection of artists studios and galleries that you may want to check out.

## UNION PARK

Where Waltham Street meets Shawmut Avenue turn left. At the next corner is the **South End Buttery**, see ⑪③. Immediately opposite is delightful **Union Park ⑪**, created in 1851, and the best-preserved of the South End's historic squares.

## BOSTON CENTER FOR THE ARTS

A few steps from Union Park's northern end is Tremont Street and the South End's highest density of restaurants. Turn right and cross the street to arrive at the **Boston Center for the Arts ⑫** (539 Tremont Street; tel: 617-426-5000; www.bcaonline.org), housing artists' studios, galleries, and four theaters.

Part of the complex is the unusual **Cyclorama**. Built in 1884 to house a gigantic circular painting (400 x 50ft/ 122 x 15m) of the Battle of Gettysburg by Paul Philippoteaux, the Cyclorama caused a sensation when it opened. The painting is now shown in Gettysburg, but the space is still used for events, and you can usually pop inside for a look.

From here head north up Clarendon Street and cross back over Columbus Avenue to find another entrance to Back Bay/South End Station.

### Why Washington is wide

If you are wondering why Washington Street is so wide, it is because it once had an elevated train line – the Washington Street 'El,' – running along it. Built at the turn of the 19th century, and one of the first of its kind in the US, the line was demolished in the 1980s to be replaced by the Orange Line of the submerged T.

---

## Food and Drink 🍴

### ② FLOUR BAKERY AND CAFÉ

1595 Washington Street, South End; tel: 617-267-4300; www.flourbakery.com; Mon–Fri 7am–9pm, Sat 8am–6pm, Sun 9am–5pm; $

The line at lunchtime nearly goes out the door for this popular café's lattes and gourmet sandwiches like lamb and curried tuna. Also at 12 Farnsworth Street (tel: 617-338-4333; Mon–Fri 7am–7pm, Sat 8am–6pm, Sun 9am–4pm), near the Children's Museum on walk 10 (see p.75).

### ③ SOUTH END BUTTERY

312 Shawmut Avenue; tel 617-482-1015; www.southendbuttery.com; Sun–Wed 6.30am–10pm, Thur–Sat 6.30am–11pm; $

Service can be sluggish at this popular corner café that specializes in great coffee, loose-leaf teas, and fresh baked goods. Pavement tables overlook Union Square. There's table service at weekend brunch and for dinner.

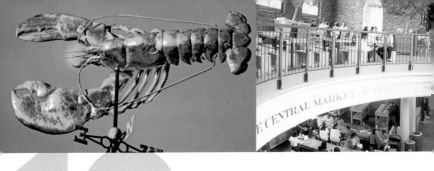

# WATERFRONT
# AND FORT POINT

*Now that the elevated expressway has been buried, Boston is rediscovering its Waterfront. Stroll along part of the HarborWalk on this route from Faneuil Hall-Quincy Market, past the fantastic New England Aquarium, to the Institute of Contemporary Art in the upcoming Fort Point district.*

**Above:** Columbus gives his name to a Waterfront park.

### Revolutionary spark

Three ships laden with tea were moored at Griffins Wharf on December 16, 1773, when patriots disguised as Mohawk Indians boarded them and threw all 340 chests of their cargo into the harbor. This was the most flamboyant act of defiance against the British Parliament for its manipulation of taxes, such as that on tea, to favor British interests. It was 'the spark that ignited the American Revolution.'

---

**DISTANCE** 3 miles (5km)
**TIME** A half day
**START** State T Station
**END** Courthouse T Station
**POINTS TO NOTE**

Allow for a full day if you plan to visit the Aquarium, the Children's Museum, and the ICA. The Children's Museum in particular will likely represent a fair outlay of time and energy for youngsters, so is best set aside as a separate destination, or at least one that follows lunch or a rest period. The weekend is a busy time to visit these places, so go on a weekday if possible. Entry to the Children's Museum is only $1 Friday 5–9pm, and the ICA is free Thursday from 5–9pm.

---

Until the second half of the 19th century Boston was the busiest port in the nation. Warehouses and counting houses occupied a dozen wharves at which clippers unloaded and loaded their cargoes. In 1878 the construction of Atlantic Avenue severed the finger-like piers from the rest of the city, a process completed with the building in the 1950s of the raised Fitzgerald

Expressway. Boston turned its back on its patrimony, and the Waterfront went into seemingly terminal decline.

A reprieve came in the 1970s with the restoration of Faneuil Hall and Quincy Market. Now that the Big Dig has buried the Expressway *(see p.13)*, the Waterfront is being rediscovered thanks to development around the Fort Point Channel and the Harbor-Walk project *(see feature, p.75)*.

## FANEUIL HALL-QUINCY MARKET

Emerge from State T Station, cross Congress Street, and dive into the retail heaven of the **Faneuil Hall-Quincy Market ❶** complex. Faneuil Hall is covered in walk 1 *(see p.30)*. Adjoining Quincy Market is named after mayor Josiah Quincy, who came up with the idea for the 1826-vintage marketplace. Meat and produce were sold here for 150 years before the buildings were renovated to host the souvenir stalls and boutiques found today. A tourist magnet, with frequent performances by buskers, Quincy Market consists of three long buildings. Eateries abound, including historic **Durgin Park**.

## COLUMBUS PARK

Leave the Quincy Market carnival behind and head toward the water, crossing the strip of park that has replaced the buried expressway to arrive at **Columbus Park ❷**. A trellised walkway leads to the Waterfront. On the left stretches **Commercial Wharf**. The massive granite warehouse here, in which the second set of sails for the USS *Constitution (see p.38)* was made, is now a condominium complex.

## LONG WHARF

Immediately to the south of Columbus Park is **Long Wharf ❸**. When built in 1710 the wharf extended from near the Old State House *(see p.29)* past the towering Custom House (now a hotel)

to the harbor. Gaze out from the esplanade at the end of the wharf to East Boston and the planes taking off from Logan Airport. Setting sail from Long Wharf is still possible, either on ferries to Provincetown *(see p.92)*, the Charlestown Navy Yard *(see p.37)*, or the Harbor Islands *(see p.76)*.

## NEW ENGLAND AQUARIUM

Beside Long Wharf is Central Wharf, on which stands the excellent **New England Aquarium ❹** (tel: 617-973-5200; www.neaq.org; Mon–Fri 9am–5pm, Sat–Sun 9am–6pm; charge). Inside, the Giant Ocean Tank rises three stories high. A ramp encircling the tank takes visitors past more than 70 wall tanks containing a plethora of weird and wonderful fish, as well as

Above from far left: lobster weather vane; rotunda at Quincy Market; Columbus Park.

Below: visit historic Durgin Park for Yankee-style cooking.

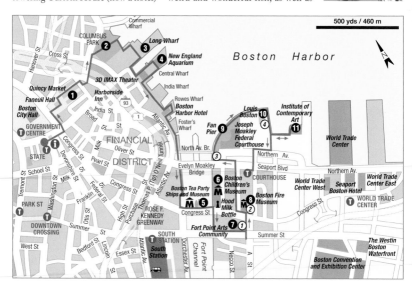

turtles and sharks. You can see three species of penguin and two varieties of seal as well. The Aquarium also runs its own whale-watching cruises *(see feature, p.77)*.

Located just across the plaza from the Aquarium is the six-story-high **3D IMAX Theater** (daily 10am–10pm; charge), which shows spectacular films of the natural world's wonders.

## Food and Drink

### ① CHANNEL CAFÉ
300 Summer Street; tel: 617-426-0695; channel-cafe.com; Mon–Fri 7am–3pm, Tue–Fri 5–10pm; $
Sharing the same building as the Fort Point Arts Community Gallery, Channel Café features mismatched furniture, freshly-cooked food including baked treats, and friendly service. There's wine and beer on tap too.

### ② SPORTELLO
348 Congress Street; tel: 617-737-1234; www.sportelloboston.com; Mon–Thur 11.30am–10pm, Fri 11.30am–11pm, Sat 10.30am–11pm, Sun 10.30am–4pm; $$
Celebrated local chef Barbara Lynch is behind this bakey café and modern interpretation of a diner: all counter seating looks onto the kitchen preparing tratorria-inspired Italian dishes. There's a groovy bar, Drink, downstairs, while Lynch's fine dining restaurant Menton *(see p.119)* is next door.

### ③ THE BARKING CRAB
Fort Point Landing, 88 Sleeper Street; tel: 617-426-2722; www.barkingcrab.com; Sun–Wed 11.30am–11pm, Thur–Sat 11.30am–1am; $$
A red-and-yellow tent covers shared bench tables at this casual shack-like place serving mainly seafood. It can get very crowded on summer evenings; if it is busy try the nearby branch of The Daily Catch *(see p.33)*.

### ④ SAM'S
225 Northern Avenue; tel: 617-330-7430; samsatlouis.com; Mon–Thur 11.30am–10pm, Fri–Sat 11.30am–11pm, Sun 11am–9pm; $$$
Slick Sam's gets it all right offering the best of French brasserie and American diner style dining with wonderful views across the harbor. Enjoy garlic roasted chicken, steak and fries or pan-seared halibut. There's live music on Friday's from 9pm.

## BOSTON TEA PARTY SHIPS AND MUSEUM

From Central Wharf continue south past India and Rowes wharves, the latter home to the swish Boston Harbor Hotel *(see p.113)*.

Fort Point Channel now intersects the Waterfront. This area was the bustling transfer point for many New England industries during the latter years of the 19th century.

Staying on the Downtown side of the channel, continue past the pedestrian Northern Avenue Bridge and Evelyn Moakley Bridge to the Congress Street Bridge. On a short wharf in the middle of the bridge are the new **Boston Tea Party Ships and Museum ⑤** (www.bostonteapartyship.com; charge), scheduled to reopen in summer 2012, when it will include full-size replicas of the tall ships *Dartmouth* and *Eleanor*, and the restored brig *Beaver*.

## CHILDREN'S MUSEUM

On the eastern side of Congress Street Bridge the iconic giant **Hood Milk Bottle** *(see p.14)* stands outside the fantastic **Boston Children's Museum ⑥** (300 Congress Street; tel: 617-426-6500; www.bostonchildrensmuseum.org; daily 10am–5pm, Fri until 9pm; charge). Hands-on installations, including a three-story climbing sculpture and many games, will thrill kids of all ages. Also here is a complete two-story Japanese silk merchant's home, a gift from Kyoto, Boston's sister city.

Follow the Fort Point Channel footpath south to Summer Street, turn right and continue down to **Channel Café**, see ⑪①, in the **Fort Point Arts Community (FPAC) Gallery** ❼ building (www.fortpointarts.org; Mon 9am–3.30pm, Tue–Fri 9am–9pm).

### BOSTON FIRE MUSEUM

Cross the street from the FPAC Gallery to find the stairs leading down to A Street. Turn left at the bottom and left again on to Congress Street. Dead ahead is **Sportello**, see ⑪②, while on the corner with Farnsworth Street the **Boston Fire Museum** ❽ (tel: 617-338-9700; bostonfiremuseum.com; Sat 11am–6pm; free) occupies a firehouse dating back to 1891. Inside are gleaming antique fire engines and other apparatus.

Further along Farnsworth Street is a branch of the café **Flour** *(see p.71)* and **Made in Fort Point**; **The FPAC Store** (tel: 617-423-1100; Mon–Fri 11am–6pm, Sat 11am–4pm) showcasing pieces by the many artists and craftspeople who live and work in the area. At the end of Farnsworth, cross Seaport Boulevard to reach **The Barking Crab**, see ⑪③, between the Evelyn Moakley and Northern Avenue bridges.

### INSTITUTE OF CONTEMPORARY ART

From here follow the water's edge north past the Joseph Moakley Federal Courthouse. This used to be **Fan Pier** ❾, so called because of the railway sidings that radiated out to the curved seawall: a small bronze model shows what it once looked like, as you approach uber-chic fashion and homegoods store **Louis-Boston** ❿ (www.louisboston.com) above which you'll find **Sam's**, see ⑪④.

Beyond LouisBoston you can't miss the **Institute of Contemporary Art** ⓫ (100 Northern Avenue; tel: 617-927-6613; www.ica boston.org; Tue–Sun 10am–5pm, Thur–Fri 10am–9pm; charge) housed in a dramatic cantilevered structure. There are some really innovative, challenging exhibitions here and a panoramic view back to Downtown from the museum's forecourt.

Silver Line buses from the nearby Courthouse T Station will take you back to the city center.

**Above from far left:** Rowes Wharf; at the New England Aquarium; Custom House; exhibit at the Institute of Contemporary Art.

**Below:** Boston Children's Museum.

## HarborWalk

The HarborWalk (www.bostonharborwalk.com) stretches 47 miles (76km) from Chelsea Creek, north of Boston, through Charlestown, North End, Downtown, and South Boston to south of Dorchester. Designed to provide access to the restored Boston Harbor, the route hugs the coastline using established walkways as well as new paths. Nearly 39 miles (63km) of the route, also suitable to cycle, have been completed. You can download audio tours from the website to listen to as you follow the route, marked by a blue line.

# HARBOR ISLANDS

*A summer trip to one or several of the 17 islands in the Boston Harbor Islands National Recreation Area promises a blissful escape from the city to discover nature and historic monuments that few Bostonians know about.*

**DISTANCE** 7 miles (11km)

**TIME** A full day

**START/END** Aquarium
T Station/Long Wharf

**POINTS TO NOTE**

The above distance is from Boston to Georges Island. Boston's Best Cruises (tel: 617-770-0040; www.bostonhar borislands.org) runs ferries to the islands from Long Wharf ($14) from early May to mid-October. It takes 30 minutes to reach Georges Island from where Lovells, Peddocks, Grape, and Bumpkin islands are between 15 to 30 minutes away using the inter-island shuttle ($5). Alternatively, go straight to Spectacle Island (15min) from where it is possible to connect to Georges.

### Camping

Three islands – Lovells, Grape, Peddocks and Bumpkin – allow camping from late June to early September for a small fee. Reservations should be made with the Department of Conservation and Recreation (tel: 617-626-1480, toll free: 1-877-422-6762; www.reserve america.com).

Boston Harbor is dotted with 34 islands, 17 of which are protected within a state park. They are all wonderful places to relax and enjoy crowd-free hiking, fishing, swimming, and kayaking, as well as a host of other activities. Check the calendar on the website of Boston Harbor Islands (tel: 617-223-8666; www.bostonharborislands.org) for scheduled events, ranging from shows by the Boston's Children's Theater, jazz performances, guided ranger walks and a boat tour around the islands that includes a visit to two historic lighthouses in the harbor.

This daytrip route, possible from mid-June to early September when the inter-island ferry operates, takes you to three of the islands: Georges, Lovell, and Spectacle. Four others – Bumpkin, Grape, Hull, and Peddocks – are also accessible on the inter-island ferry, while others, such as Little Brewster, can be reached by ferries direct from the city.

### GEORGES ISLAND

From the Aquarium T Station walk the short distance west to **Long Wharf ①**, where you can board the 9am ferry to Georges Island. The gateway to the other Harbor Islands, **Georges Island ②** is also the site of Fort Warren, built in 1833; take one of the ranger-led tours

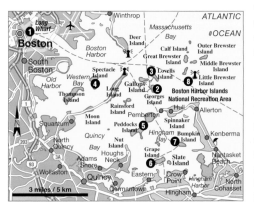

around the abandoned complex that once was a training ground for Union soldiers and a prison for Confederate captives. There is a large picnic area here (with restrooms and a snack bar), as well as magnificent views of the Boston skyline and surrounding islands.

## LOVELLS ISLAND

Board the 11.35am inter-island ferry from Georges to **Lovells Island** ❸. Here you can explore the ruins of Fort Standish, search out diverse wildlife, relax on inviting beaches, and wander rocky shores upon which several ships were wrecked. Lovells is one of three islands on which camping is permitted.

## SPECTACLE ISLAND

Take the 2.55pm inter-island ferry back to Georges, switching to the 3.30pm ferry for **Spectacle Island** ❹. This is the closest of the park's islands to the city and features a marina, visitor center, café, and life-guarded swimming beach. Follow part of the island's 5 miles (8km) of walking trails that lead to the top of a 157ft (48m) hill offering panoramic views. There are direct ferries from Spectacle Island to Long Wharf and vice versa.

## OTHER ISLANDS

Around a mile south of Georges lies **Peddocks Island** ❺, the third-largest harbor island, which has many walking trails, and the remains of Fort Andrews built under the shadow of the Spanish-

American War, and garrisoned during World Wars I and II.

**Grape Island** ❻ has a campsite, and offers trails along which you are sure to see wildlife and birds among the wild berry trees. Camping is also allowed on **Bumpkin Island** ❼, which lies close to the Hull Peninsula, and hosts the remains of a children's hospital and a farmhouse overgrown with vegetation such as bayberries and wild raspberries.

Only open for tours (for schedule see www.bostonharborislands.org/tour-lighthouse) **Little Brewster** ❽ is home to Boston Light, the first and oldest lighthouse in the US. The present building was constructed in 1782 after the British had blown up the original (built in 1716) on departing Boston in 1776. It is the only lighthouse in the nation still manned (except in winter) by resident keepers.

**Above from far left:** Graves Light; diving whale; Little Brewster and Boston Light.

**Food and drink** Bring a picnic, as the only two islands with any food or drink on them are Georges and Spectacle, both of which host snack bars during the summer season.

## Whale watching

The humpback gathering at the fertile feeding ground Stellwagen Bank, 25 miles (40km) off the Boston coast, is one of the greatest in the world. Minkie whales can be seen too. Boston Harbor Cruises (tel: 617-227-4321; www.bostonharborcruises) and New England Aquarium Whale Watch (tel: 617-973-5206; www.neaq. org) run whale-watching tours from Long and Central wharves respectively. The season starts in April and ends in October, with the peak around June. Cruises take around three hours, and commentary is provided by naturalists. The waters can be rough, so it is a good idea to carry anti-seasickness tablets. Rainwear is useful in April and May, and you should dress warmly even in summer. Whale-watching tours also depart from Gloucester (see p.83), Plymouth (see p.90), and Provincetown (see p.93).

# SALEM

*There is more to Salem, 16 miles (26km) north of Boston, than witches, as you will discover on this walk around one of New England's most historic towns, which is home to the exceptional Peabody Essex Museum, a treasure trove of art and culture from around the world.*

## Tourist information

Just off Essex Mall on New Liberty Street is the National Park Visitor Center (tel: 978-740-1650; www.nps.gov; daily 9am–5pm), where you can pick up maps and leaflets, consult the park rangers, and watch an excellent 25-minute film about the county's history. Tourist information is also available at www.salem.org.

**DISTANCE** 3½ miles (5.5km)
**TIME** A full day
**START/END** Salem Station
**POINTS TO NOTE**

The distance above is that of the walking route around Salem. To get to Salem (16 miles/26km north of Boston), take a train from the city's North Station (22 minutes; $5.50) on the Newburyport/Rockport Commuter Rail Line (www.mbta.com). Alternatively, from May to October ferries run from Central Wharf next to the New England Aquarium in Boston to Blaney Street Wharf in Salem (tel: 978-741-0220; www.bostonsbest cruises.com/salem-ferry; one way/round-trip $13/24). The voyage by ferry takes 45 minutes.

Salem – the name derives from the Hebrew *shalom* (peace) – was once one of the nation's great seaports. It produced the country's first millionaires, and has the architectural and cultural heritage to prove it in its McIntire Historic District and the protected properties of the Peabody Essex Museum. However, it does not take long to find reminders of the activities most often associated with the town – the trials and executions of 'witches.'

## WITCH DUNGEON MUSEUM

Starting from **Salem Station**, ascend the steps at the end of the platform, cross the busy road, and walk down Washington Street, turning right onto Lynde Street after two blocks. At no. 16

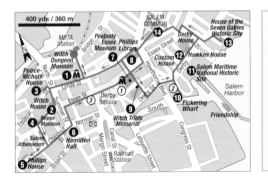

## Food and Drink

① RED'S SANDWICH SHOP
15 Central Street; tel: 978-745-3257; www.redssandwichshop.com; Mon–Sat 5am–3pm, Sun 6am–1pm; $
A Salem breakfast institution housed in the old London Coffee House, dating from 1698. Arrive early if you don't want to stand in line. You can also get grilled sandwiches – great for a lunchtime snack.

is the **Witch Dungeon Museum** (tel: 978-741-3570; www.witchdun geon.com; daily Apr–Nov 10am–5pm; charge), where you can watch a vividly staged re-enactment of a trial, adapted from a 1692 manuscript, before being guided through the tiny dank dungeons in which the accused were held.

### Witch House

The nearby spooky wooden house on the corner of Essex and North streets is the **Witch House** ❷ (tel: 978-744-8815 www.salemweb.com/witchhouse; mid-May–Nov daily 10am–5pm; charge), where trial magistrate Jonathan Corwin cross-examined more than 200 suspected witches; the decor is authentic to the period.

## MCINTIRE HISTORIC DISTRICT

Named after Samuel McIntire (1757–1811), one of the foremost American architects of his day, this historic area of Salem, roughly bounded by Federal, Flint, Broad, and Summer/North streets, showcases four centuries of architectural styles.

### Historic houses

Backtrack from the Witch House to Federal Street, where at no. 80 stands the McIntire-designed **Peirce-Nichols House** ❸ (*c*.1782). The house's restored east parlor is open for tours by arrangement with the Peabody Essex Museum.

Return to Essex Street and proceed to no. 318, the Georgian-period **Ropes**

Mansion ❹, which stands in a beautiful garden (free), and features a rare collection of Nanking porcelain and Irish glass. Across the road at no. 337 is the **Salem Athenaeum** (www.salem athenaeum.net; Tue–Wed and Fri 1–5pm, Thur 5–9pm, Sat 10am–2pm; free), a library formed from two previous libraries in 1810.

Turn into quaint Botts Court and walk to Chestnut Street, one of Salem's finest thoroughfares. At no. 34 is the elegant **Phillips House** ❺ (tel: 978-744-0440; www.historicnewengland. org; June–Oct Tue–Sun 10am–4pm; charge) where the carriage house contains several antique cars. Retrace your steps back along Chestnut Street to no. 9, the red-brick Federalist gem **Hamilton Hall** ❻ (www.hamilton hall.org). now used for weddings and other events.

## PEABODY ESSEX MUSEUM

From the corner of Chestnut Street turn left onto Summer Street and then right at Essex Street to reach the pedestrian Essex Mall, recognizable by the red paving that matches the red bricks of the buildings. Turn right onto Central Street for **Red's Sandwich Shop**, see ⑪①.

Back on the Mall, reserve a decent block of time to visit the outstanding **Peabody Essex Museum** ❼ (tel: 978-745-9500; pem.org; daily 10am–5pm; charge), where an impressive contemporary building by Moshe Safdie displays a fraction of the collection of nearly a million objects.

## Historic houses

It is possible to look inside several of the houses in the McIntire Historic District and elsewhere around town by arrangement with the Peabody Essex Museum *(see p.79)*, which manages 22 buildings around Salem, including those in the Phillips Library Neighborhood opposite the museum's main building.

The museum's origins date back to 1799 and to the art and antiques amassed by Salem's seafaring merchants on their global travels. Ships' models, figureheads, nautical instruments, charts, and maps abound, but the museum also has fine antiques from China, Japan, and India, as well as plenty of artifacts from the South Pacific (especially the Solomon Islands) and further afield. There is also a 200-year-old Chinese merchant's home transported from China and rebuilt as part of the museum; entry to this is by timed ticket, and advance reservations are advised.

### PHILLIPS LIBRARY

Diagonally opposite the Peabody Essex Museum, a mini architectural park surrounds the red-brick **Phillips Library** ❽ (tel: 978-745-9500; pem.org; Wed 10am–5pm, Thur 1–5pm; free), which has a lovely reading room. Notice the stark contrast between the massive columns of the **Andrew-Safford House** (1819; 13 Washington Square) and, behind it, the tiny features of the **Derby-Beebe Summerhouse** (1799). Also here are the **Gardner-Pingree House** (1804; 128 Essex Street) and, from 1727, the neighboring **Crowninshield-Bentley House**.

### WITCH TRIALS MEMORIAL

Follow the short footpath around the eastern side of the Peabody until you reach Charter Street. Here, next to the Burying Point Cemetery – resting place of witch judge John Hathorne – is the most poignant of all Salem's witch-connected sites. The **Witch Trials Memorial** ❾, dedicated by Holocaust survivor and renowned writer Elie Wiesel in 1992, is a contemplative space surrounded by 20 stone benches etched with the trial victims' names, and shaded by a clump of black locust trees – reputedly the kind from which the convicted were hanged.

### SALEM MARITIME NATIONAL HISTORIC SITE

From the cemetery, cross Derby Street and walk along its southern side toward **Pickering Wharf** ❿, a touristy collection of stores and restaurants including several antiques shops. The best place to eat here is **Finz**, see ⑪②.

Next to the wharf, the **Salem Maritime National Historic Site** ⓫ focuses on Salem's port. Stop by the **Orientation Center** (tel: 978-740-1660; www.nps.gov; daily 9am–5pm)

## Salem's witch hysteria

In 1692, between June and September, Salem fell under a dark spell of mass hysteria, and executed 14 women and six men for witchcraft. You would be forgiven for thinking that the town is still obsessed with witches, for that sad history, portrayed in the Arthur Miller play *The Crucible*, is recalled at many sites – a few historical, others kitsch. Every October the town ramps up its black-arts connection further to run a month-long celebration called Haunted Happenings (www.hauntedhappenings.org), culminating in the crowning of the king and queen of Halloween on the 31st.

to find out about ranger-guided tours (charge) to the nearby Custom House, Derby House, and Narbonne House, as well as the *Friendship*, a full-scale replica of a 1797 three-masted East India merchant ship. It is docked at Derby Wharf, one of the few wharves that remain from the 40 of Salem's heyday.

## CUSTOM HOUSE

Facing the wharf is the **Custom House** ⑫ (1819), surmounted by a gilded eagle clutching in its claws arrows and a shield, which was made infamous by Nathaniel Hawthorne. Salem's most famous son worked here for three years of 'slavery,' on which he based the introduction to *The Scarlet Letter* (1850).

Adjacent to the Custom House is the **Hawkes House** (1780; not open to the public) and, beyond that, the ochre-brick **Derby House** (1761). The former was built by shipowner Elias Hasket Derby (probably America's first millionaire), to replace the latter, but it was never completed, and was used as a storehouse for booty taken by his Revolutionary privateers.

## THE HOUSE OF THE SEVEN GABLES

Continue down Derby Street from the Custom House to reach, at no. 115, **The House of the Seven Gables** ⑬ (tel: 978-744-0991; www.7gables.org; daily July–Oct 10am–7pm, Feb–June and Nov–Dec 10am–5pm; charge),

which inspired Nathaniel Hawthorne to write the novel of that name. The small house in which he was born in 1806 has been moved into the grounds. Guides lead you through rooms stuffed with period furniture. Take a breather in the lovely garden afterwards.

From Derby Street you could walk two blocks east to Blaney Street to catch the ferry back to Boston. Otherwise, you can return to Salem Station via **Salem Common** ⑭, near where you'll find the Hawthorn Hotel *(see margin, p.79)*, and the relaxed café-bar **Gulu-Gulu Café**, see ⑪③.

Above from far left: Derby House; replica of the *Friendship*; House of the Seven Gables; eagle atop the Custom House.

Left: Custom House.

---

### Food and Drink

**② FINZ**
76 Wharf Street; tel: 978-744-8485; www.hpfinz.com; daily 11.30am–midnight; $$$
The best place to enjoy seafood overlooking Salem Harbor. Prioritise the excellent salmon wrap or great-value haddock sandwich.

**③ GULU-GULU CAFE**
247 Essex Street; tel: 978-740-8882; www.gulu-gulu.com; Mon–Wed 10am–10pm, Thur–Fri 10am–1am, Sat 9am–1am, Sun 9am–10pm; $$
With outdoor seats for people watching along Essex Mall, and free wi-fi, this Czech-themed café-bar is a good place for coffee, beer or meal. Also has live music in the evening.

# CAPE ANN

*Maritime history, artists' colonies, grand New England mansions, and spectacular coastal scenery are among the attractions of Cape Ann, which is an easy day's drive northeast from Boston.*

### Place to stay

The Addison Choate Inn (49 Broadway, Rockport; tel: 1800-245-7543; www. addisonchoateinn. com) is a charming 1850s house that offers modern conveniences such as Wi-Fi. It has six rooms, and there is a separate cottage with two self-catering units.

### Tourist information

Online tourist information is available at www.seecape ann.com, www.cape annvacations.com, and www.rockport usa.com.

**Below:** cry of the gull.

---

**DISTANCE** 40 miles (63km) from Boston to Rockport

**TIME** A full day

**START** Gloucester

**END** Rockport

**POINTS TO NOTE**

Driving is the best way to get around Cape Ann; the fastest way from Boston is along Route 128, while the most scenic is along MA 127, which follows the coast beyond Salem. Both Gloucester and Rockport are accessible by train from Boston's North Station, and you can get around on Cape Ann Transportation Authority buses (www.canntran.com; tel: 978-283-7916).

---

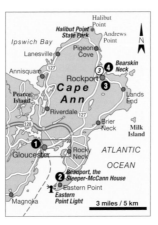

---

## GLOUCESTER

Founded in 1623 by English fishermen, **Gloucester ❶** is the nation's oldest seaport. Unlike Salem, its harbor is still fairly active, with many fishermen now of Portuguese or Italian descent.

If you head into Gloucester along Route 127 from the west, just over the drawbridge spanning the Annisquam Canal you will see the **Fisherman's Monument ❹**, with a helmsman gripping a wheel as he scans the horizon.

### Cape Ann Museum

In town begin at **Cape Ann Museum ❸** (27 Pleasant Street; tel: 978-283-0455; www.capeannmuseum.org; Tue–Sat 10am–5pm, Sun 1–4pm; charge), displaying seascapes by the American maritime painter Fitz Hugh Lane and an interesting collection of furniture, silver, and porcelain, in the home of Captain Elias Davis (1804) and the adjoining White-Ellery House (*c.*1709).

Walk west along Middle Street, at no. 49, is the **Sargent House Museum ❻** (tel: 978-281-2432; sargenthouse.org; late May–early Sept Fri–Sun noon–4pm; charge), the home of Judith Sargent and John Murray, where rooms are arranged as they might have been in 1782 when the house was built. A block south, toward the harbor, you will find

several lunch options on Main Street, including **Passports**, see ①. Further along is **Alchemy**, see ②, a convivial spot to return to in the evening.

Further inland, on Main Street, is the attractive Portuguese **Church of Our Lady of Good Voyage** **D**, recognizable by its two blue cupolas.

*Rocky Neck and Eastern Point*

From the church, drive around the harbor to East Main Street, off of which a road leads to **Rocky Neck** **E** (www.rockyneckartcolony.org), the oldest artists' colony in the US, in a wonderful coastal setting. Rudyard Kipling worked on *Captains Courageous*, about Gloucester fishermen, while staying here.

On leaving Rocky Neck, turn right onto Eastern Point Road. After about 1 mile (1.6km), take the right fork, even though it is marked 'private.' This is the exclusive enclave of Eastern Point. Open to the public is **Beauport, the Sleeper-McCann House** **2** (tel: 978-283-0800; www.historicnewengland.org; June–mid-Oct Tue–Sat 10am–last tour at 4pm; charge), built and furnished between 1907 and 1934 by Henry Davis Sleeper, a collector of American art and antiquities. On the tour you can see rooms Sleeper decorated to cover different periods of American life.

## ROCKPORT

About 7 miles (11km) northeast of Gloucester is picturesque **Rockport** **3**, once a shipping center for locally cut granite. In the 1920s Rockport was discovered by artists; it remains an art colony today. A dozen galleries display works of both local and international artists on Main Street, but what attracts most tourists is **Bearskin Neck** **4**. This narrow peninsula, jutting out beyond the harbor, is packed with tiny dwellings and old fishing sheds, now converted into galleries, antiques stores, and restaurants. Enjoy magnificent views of the Atlantic from the breakwater at the end of the Neck, just before which you will pass **My Place by the Sea**, see ①③.

Above from far left: Gloucester harbor; colorful fishing floats; a photographers' favorite in Rockport is a red lobster shack, visible from Dock Square, called 'Motif No. 1' because of the infinite number of times it has been photographed and painted.

**Whale watching**
Cape Ann Whale Watch (tel: 1-800-877-5110; www.seethewhales.com) runs whale-watching cruises from Rose Wharf, Gloucester.

## Food and Drink

① **PASSPORTS**
110 Main Street, Gloucester; tel: 978-281-3680; passports restaurant.wordpress.com; Mon–Fri 11.30am–9pm, Sat 8am–10pm, Sun 8am–9.30pm; $
Romantically themed café; great salads, soups, and seafood.

② **ALCHEMY**
3 Duncan Street, Gloucester; tel: 978-281-3997; www.alchemy bistro.com; Mon–Thur 11.30am–4pm, 5pm–9pm, Fri 11.30am–4pm, 5pm–10pm, Sat 10.30am–4pm, 5pm–10pm, Sun 10.30am–4pm, 5pm–9pm; $$
This convivial bistro serves a good range of on-tap real ales, wines and cocktails, as well as tapas plates designed for sharing.

③ **MY PLACE BY THE SEA**
68 Bearskin Neck, Rockport; 978-546-9667; daily May–early Dec 11.30am–3pm; $$
Fantastic views are guaranteed at this adorable, friendly place serving imaginative modern American cuisine. Good value for lunch, pricier for dinner, when reservations are advised.

# LEXINGTON AND CONCORD

*Following the 'Battle Road' between Lexington and Concord, west of Boston, will take you past key Revolutionary sites, as well as the beautiful landscape and classic New England locations that inspired American literary giants.*

**Public transport**
From Boston's Alewife T Station you can take bus no. 62 or 76 to Lexington center. From spring through fall the Liberty Ride tour *(see margin, p.86)* covers the 7 miles (11km) between Lexington and Concord. Alternatively, take a taxi; try Yellow Cabs (tel: 781-862-4600). Trains from Lincoln, a 4-mile (6.5km) walk south-west from Concord, go to Boston's North Station (40 minutes).

**DISTANCE** 13 miles (20½km) from Boston to Lexington
**TIME** A full day
**START** National Heritage Museum, Lexington
**END** DeCordova Museum and Sculpture Park, Lincoln
**POINTS TO NOTE**
In a car you can visit all the sites in this tour in a day. Consider spending the night in Concord, if you wish to linger at any of the museums or hike the Battle Road Trail. Many sites are shut Sun morning and Nov–mid-April.

## LEXINGTON

To reach the start of this tour, head out of Boston on Route 2. Turn right at exit 57 onto Route 4-225. As you approach the center of Lexington there are two sites of historical interest on the left.

### National Heritage Museum
A contemporary building houses the **National Heritage Museum ❶** (33 Marrett Road; tel: 781-861-6559; www.monh.org; Wed– Sat 10am–4.30pm free), which features changing exhibits of Americana across four centuries.

## Food and Drink 🍴

### ① VIA LAGO
1845 Massachusetts Avenue, Lexington; tel: 781-861-6174; www.vialogocatering.com; Mon–Wed 7am–9pm, Thur–Sat 7am–9.30pm; $
Freshly made sandwiches, light meals, and other snacks are available from this convivial café, which is situated within sight of Battle Green.

### ② YANGTZE RIVER
25 Depot Square, Lexington; tel: 781-861-6030; www.yangtze lexington.com; Sun–Thur 11.30am–9.15pm, Fri–Sat 11.30am–10.15pm; $
Lexington has a large Chinese population; the fact that many of them frequent this restaurant proves how good the food is. Their dim sum and all-you-can eat buffet brunch at the weekend is a steal at $13.95 per person.

Soon after is the 1635 **Munroe Tavern ❷** (1332 Massachusetts Avenue; tel: 781-862-1703; www.lexington history.org; daily June–Oct noon–4pm, hourly tours; charge), which served as headquarters for the Redcoats and as a hospital on their retreat from Concord.

*Battle Green*

Drive into the center and park. At one corner of the town common, a tiny triangular park known as **Battle Green ❸**, stands the **Minuteman Statue**, honoring the 77 patriots who faced down the British here, igniting the American Revolution of 1775. They were called Minutemen because they pledged to be ready to fight at a minute's notice.

Opposite on Bedford Street is **Buckman Tavern ❹** (daily April–Oct 10am–4pm, tours every half-hour; charge), a clapboard building that has been restored to its late 17th-century appearance. After the first battle of the Revolution, wounded Minutemen

were brought here for medical attention. Check out the bullet holes in the door, muskets, original cooking equipment, and 17th-century furniture.

A short walk northwest from Battle Green is **Hancock-Clarke House ❺** (36 Hancock Street; April–May Sat–Sun 10am–4pm, daily June–Oct 10am–4pm, hourly tours; charge). This house is where, on the night of April 18, 1771, Paul Revere awoke John Hancock and Samuel Adams to warn that the British were coming.

Before leaving Lexington you could get some refreshments at **Via Lago**, see ⑪①, facing Battle Green, or **Yangtze River**, see ⑪②, around the corner.

## BATTLE ROAD

Drive out of Lexington west on Massachusetts Avenue to join Route 2A which shadows **Battle Road ❻**, along which the British, harried by the Minutemen, marched toward Concord.

### Revolution

The battles that started the American Revolution of 1775, leading up to the Declaration of Independence the following year, began in these neighboring villages, where the Minutemen – a militia of rebels against British rule – faced off against His Majesty's armies, the Redcoats. The first skirmish, at Lexington, did not go well for the Patriots, with eight Minutemen killed. Eleven Redcoats, however, were casualties at Concord.

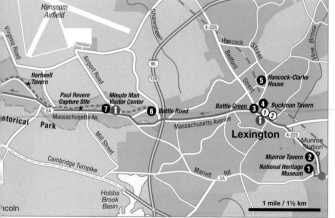

### Tourist information

Lexington Visitor Center (1875 Massachusetts Avenue; tel: 781-862-1450; www. lexingtonchamber. org; daily Dec–Mar 10am–4pm, Apr–Nov 9am–5pm) is opposite Battle Green next to Buckman Tavern.

## The Liberty Ride

On Saturday and Sunday from mid-April to early May and then daily until mid-October, the Liberty Ride (tel: 781-862-0500; www.tour lexington.us/libertyride. html; $25) tour bus travels between Lexington and Concord, visiting the key historic sites along the route. It is a 90-minute continuous loop guided tour, and you can hop on and off at the various stops as you please within a 48-hour period.

This whole area is preserved in the Minute Man National Historical Park, which has an easy 5-mile (8km) **walking trail** *(see dotted line, map)*. Stop off at the **Minute Man Visitor Center ❼** (tel: 978-318-7832; www.nps.gov/mima; daily mid-Mar–Oct 9am–5pm, Nov until 4pm; free; parking free) to see an excellent multimedia presentation about the start of the Revolution.

### CONCORD

The handsome small town of Concord is doubly important; it was the site of the second engagement of the Revolution and also the home of renowned literati in the first half of the 19th century.

### Literary homes

On the way into Concord is **The Wayside ❽** (455 Lexington Road; tel: 978-318-7826; www.nps.gov/mima; guided tours mid-May–Aug Wed–Sun, Sept–Oct Fri–Sun, phone for tour times; charge). Louisa May Alcott and her family lived here, as did Nathaniel Hawthorne in the last years of his life. Most of the furnishings, though, date from the residence of Margaret Sidney, the author of *Five Little Peppers*.

Down the road, at No. 399, is **Orchard House ❾** (tel: 978-369-4118; www.lousiamayalcott.org; Nov–Mar Mon–Fri 11am–3pm, Sat 10am–4.30pm, Apr–Oct Mon–Sat 10am–4.30pm, year-round Sun 1–4.30pm; charge), the Alcott family home from 1858 to 1877, where Louisa wrote *Little Women* and her father, Bronson, founded his school of philosophy.

### Concord Museum

Where Lexington Road meets the Cambridge Turnpike is the splendid **Concord Museum ❿** (tel: 978-369-9763; www.concordmuseum.org; Mon–Sat 9am–5pm, Sun noon–5pm; charge). It contains one of the lanterns that were hung in the Old North Church to warn that the Redcoats were leaving for Concord and Lexington. You can also see Ralph Waldo Emerson's study, which was transferred pretty much in its entirety from the Emerson House across the road. The museum also has the largest collection of artifacts associated with the author Henry David Thoreau, including the writing desk from his Walden Pond abode.

### Monument Square

Around ¼ mile (400m) further west is **Monument Square ⓫**, the heart of Concord. On the square's eastern side is the **Colonial Inn**, see ⑪③.

---

## Food and Drink

### ③ COLONIAL INN

48 Monument Square, Concord; tel: 978-369-9200; www.concordscolonialinn.com; daily 7am–9pm; $$
Dating back to 1716, this is as traditional as it gets in Concord, although all but 15 of the hotel's 60 rooms are in a modern brick annex. Rates start at $200 per night. Meals are available throughout the day, but book at least 24 hours in advance for their formal high tea ($25) served Sat and Sun 3–5pm.

### ④ MAIN STREETS MARKET AND CAFÉ

42 Main Street, Concord; tel: 978-369-9948; www.mainstreetsmarketandcafe.com; Mon 6.30am– 6pm, Tue–Thur 6.30am–10.30pm, Fri–Sat 6.30am–11.30pm; $
Bustling self-serve hangout during the day, when it is probably best to grab a delicious cake and coffee to go and enjoy them down at Walden Pond. Live music most evenings.

Park your car, and from the square take a stroll east along Bedford Street (Route 62) to reach **Sleepy Hollow Cemetery** ⓬. In an idyllic setting in the northeastern corner of the cemetery lies Authors' Ridge, the final resting place of Hawthorne, the Alcotts, Emerson, and Thoreau.

### Old Manse

Return to Monument Square and drive north for about a mile (nearly 2km) on Monument Street to arrive at the **Old Manse** ⓭ (tel: 978-369-3909; thetrustees.org; mid-Feb–mid Apr Sat–Sun noon–4pm, mid-Apr–Oct Mon–Sat 10am–5pm, Sun noon–5pm; charge), set in immaculate grounds. From this 1770 building the Rev. William Emerson watched the battle for nearby Old North Bridge in 1775. It was later the residence of his grandson, Ralph Waldo Emerson, and then, for three years after their wedding, the Hawthornes.

### Old North Bridge

From the Old Manse, stroll to the replica **Old North Bridge** ⓮, spanning the Concord River. On the other side stands the **Minuteman Statue**, rifle in one hand, ploughshare in the other. Emerson's immortal words, 'The shot heard 'round the world,' are inscribed on the plinth. On a hill overlooking the bridge is the **North Bridge Visitor Center** (tel: 978-369-6993; daily 9am–5pm).

Return to the centre of Concord and Main Street to find **Main Streets Market and Café**, see ⑪④.

## WALDEN POND

From here, travel south out of town along Walden Street, which crosses Route 2, for 1½ miles (2½ km) to hit **Walden Pond** ⓯ (parking charge), which inspired Thoreau's memoir *Walden* (1854). It takes about an hour to circle the relatively small pond on foot. The best time to visit is in the fall. During summer the pond is a popular swimming spot. A cairn of stones stands alongside the site where the writer lived in a cabin between 1845 and 1847.

## GROPIUS HOUSE

Continue south from Walden Pond and, after half a mile, turn left on Baker Bridge Road to reach at no. 68 the **Gropius House** ⓰ (tel: 781-259-8098; www.historicnewengland.org; June–mid-Oct Wed–Sun 11am–4pm, rest of year Sat–Sun only; tours on the hour; charge). This was the first building the German architect designed on arriving in the US in 1937; it expresses Bauhaus principles of function and simplicity.

## DECORDOVA MUSEUM AND SCULPTURE PARK

Another mile or so leads to the superb **deCordova Museum and Sculpture Park** ⓱ (51 Sandy Pond Road, Lincoln; tel: 781-259-8355; www.decordova.org; sculpture park daily 7am–7pm; museum Tue–Sun 11am–5pm; charge), showcasing temporary exhibitions of modern art and sculpture in 35 acres (14 hectares) of splendid grounds.

**Above from far left:** demonstrating the firing of a musket; Walden Pond; Colonial Inn.

### Places to stay

Apart from Concord's Colonial Inn (*see Food and Drink, left*), another highly recommended overnight-stay option is the delightfully decorated Hawthorne Inn (462 Lexington Road; tel: 978-369-5610; www.concordmass.com), in an 1870s house opposite The Wayside.

**Below:** Thoreau; replica of the author's cabin.

# PLYMOUTH

*Head south of Boston to Plymouth to see the spot where 102 pilgrims landed in December 1620, a replica of the ship on which they sailed, and a living recreation of the village in which they dwelt.*

### Getting around

GATRA buses can get you around Plymouth's further-flung sites, but a more convenient option is to take a taxi: try Seabreeze (tel: 508-888-0774), Patriot Cabs (tel: 508-747-1702, or South Shore Taxi (tel: 508-406-8908). From May to September you can take a narrated trolley bus tour (tel: 508-746-0378; www. p-b.com/ahs.html) of the town's major sites on the hour daily between 10am and 4pm, starting at Plymouth Rock.

**Below:** Jenney Grist Mill.

---

**DISTANCE** 40 miles (64km) from Boston to Plymouth; walk: 1½ miles (2.5km)
**TIME** A full day
**START/END** Plymouth Waterfront Tourist Information Center
**POINTS TO NOTE**

If driving, head south out of Boston along Route 1-93, then Route 3, taking exit 6A for Plymouth center. There are direct trains to Plymouth, but the service is very limited and the station is about 2 miles (3km) from the town center. It is better to take one of the more frequent trains to Kingston, from where GATRA buses (tel: 1800-483-2500; www.gatra.org) run to the corner of Memorial Drive and Court Street in Plymouth's center. Alternatively, Plymouth and Brockton buses (tel: 508-746-0378; www.p-b.com) run from Boston to Plymouth's bus depot, just off Route 3 around 2 miles (3km) southwest of Plymouth Rock.

---

Named after the port town in England from where the Pilgrims had sailed, Plymouth (originally spelled Plimoth) was the first permanent settlement in New England. It initially proved a benighted home for the immigrants, about half of whom died in the first winter though

starvation and exposure to the elements. Only with the aid of the Native American tribes did the remaining settlers survive and begin to prosper, leading to the first Thanksgiving festival after the successful harvest of 1621.

## AROUND PILGRIM MEMORIAL STATE PARK

Begin at the **Waterfront Tourist Information Center ❶** *(see margin, right)*, then proceed south along Water Street toward **Pilgrim Memorial State Park ❷**. The park's focus is **Plymouth Rock**, an underwhelming boulder that was identified in 1741 by a third-generation elder of the Plymouth Church as the rock upon which the Pilgrim Fathers first stepped, in December 1620, on reaching America. Today this mythical site is protected within a classical portico.

### Mayflower II

A mere stone's throw from the monument is the ***Mayflower II* ❸** (tel: 508-746-1622; www.plimoth.org; Apr–Nov daily 9am–5pm; charge). This boat, a replica of the original *Mayflower*, was built in England, and sailed to Plymouth in 1957. The 104ft (32m) long vessel vividly conveys the hardships that the 102 members of the crew suffered during the original 55-day voyage.

## Cole's Hill

Across the road from Plymouth Rock, climb the stone steps up **Cole's Hill ❹** where, during their first winter on the continent, the Pilgrims buried their deceased in the dead of night. These were not marked, 'lest the Indians know how many were the graves.' Over the centuries erosion revealed some of these unmarked graves, and the remains were placed in a sarcophagus atop the hill.

Near the sarcophagus is a fine bronze statue of **Massasoit**, the Wampanoag chief who befriended the Pilgrims, gave them food, and taught them to plant indigenous vegetables.

### BESIDE THE TOWN BROOK

Return to Water Street and continue south to nearby **Brewster Gardens ❺**, a pretty park that hugs both sides of the **Town Brook** from which first the Native Americans and, later, the British settlers got their fresh water and herring.

## Jenney Grist Mill

Cross the wooden bridge and follow the brook under two road bridges to arrive at **Jenney Grist Mill ❻** (6 Spring Lane; tel: 508-747-4544; www.jenneygrist mill.org; April–end-Nov Mon, Tue, Thur–Sat 9.30am– 5pm, Sun 1–5pm; charge), located on the site of the mill established in 1636 by John Jenney. Corn is still ground here as it was in the Pilgrims' time.

## Richard Sparrow House

Turn right off Spring Lane onto Summer Street to find, at no. 42, the oldest home in Plymouth. The **Richard Sparrow House ❼** (tel: 508-747-1240; www.sparrowhouse.com; Apr–Dec Thur–Tue 10am–5pm; charge), dates from 1640 and is set up so you can see how the early settlers lived. Next door, Sparrow House Pottery offers a colorful range of crafts.

### BURIAL HILL

Follow Summer Street to Market Street and turn left into the Town Square, passing the white clapboard building (dating from 1749) that served as the Court House for Plymouth County; it is now a missable museum. Opposite, also recognizable by its white wooden

**Above from far left:**
*Mayflower II*; Union flag atop the ship; Plymouth Rock; clapboard townhouses.

**Tourist information**
The Waterfront Tourist Information Center (170 Water Street; tel: 508-747-7533; www. visit-plymouth.com; Apr–Nov 9am–5pm, June–Aug 9am–8pm) is the best place to start your exploration of Plymouth; pick up maps, information about what's on, and even an MP3 player ($5) for a guided walk around the town.

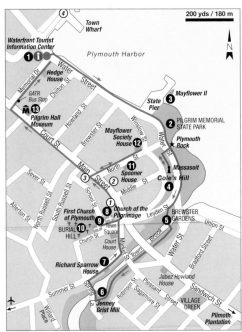

## Whale watching

For a whale-watching trip from Plymouth try Captain John Boats (tel: 1-800-242-2469; www.captjohn.com). The Captain also runs a daily ferry to and from Provincetown (see p.92) between the end of June and the beginning of September.

structure, is the **Church of the Pilgrimage** ❽. Standing between them is the stone-built **First Church of Plymouth** ❾, the longest continually active church in the US.

**Burial Hill** ❿ (dawn to dusk) rises up behind the First Church. Many of the first settlers, including William Bradford, and John and Priscilla Alden, were buried here. It is also the site of the Pilgrims' first meeting house, watchtower, and fort, whose cannons protected the harbor. There is a good view of the town and harbor from the top of the hill.

## Food and Drink

① KISKADEE COFFEE COMPANY

18 Main Street; tel: 508-830-1410; www.kiskadeecoffee.com; Mon–Fri 6.30am–5pm, Sat–Sun 7.30am– 5pm; $

They do coffee here, of course, but also a big range of bagel and panini sandwiches, as well as other tempting freshly baked goods. Free internet is also a plus.

② SAM DIEGO'S

51 Main Street; tel: 508-747-0048; www.samdiegos.com; daily 11.30am–1am; $$

Enjoy tasty Mexican and southwestern cuisine on the terrace of this lively restaurant (housed in a former fire station), and watch the passing parade on Main Street.

③ ALL THINGS TEA

20 Court Street; tel: 508-747-1221; www.allthingstea.net; Wed–Sun noon–5pm; $

A genteel, traditional English-style temple to tea, fitting for this original Pilgrim settlement. Enjoy warm scones with a pot from their wide choice of teas and infusions, or opt for the full afternoon tea if you are hungrier.

④ LOBSTER HUT

25 Town Wharf; tel: 508-746-2270; www.lobsterhutplymouth.com Sun–Thur 11am–8pm, Fri–Sat 11am–9pm; $

Really nothing fancy, but when it comes to enjoying seafood within toe-dipping-distance of the water, then this Plymouth institution is the place to head.

## LUNCH ON MAIN STREET

Head back downhill to Main Street, Plymouth's central shopping street, where you can turn left to find **Kiskadee Coffee Company**, see ⊗①, and across the road, **Sam Diego's**, see ⊗②.

## HISTORIC HOUSES

Take the second right onto North Street. At no. 27 is **Spooner House** ⓫ (tel: 508-746-0012; June–Sept Thur–Fri 2–6pm, Sat 9am–noon; charge), dating from 1749. This is one of three historical houses in town managed by the Plymouth Antiquarian Society, and features 18th-century furnishings and the belongings of the Spooner family, who lived here for two centuries.

### Mayflower Society House

Across the road is the impressive white-washed **Mayflower Society House** ⓬ (tel: 508-746-2590; www.themayflowersociety.com; mid–June–early Oct daily 11am–4pm, early June and mid–late Oct Sat–Sun only; charge), dating back to 1754. Tours of the interior, reflecting the occupants down the centuries, while behind the house is a library for genealogical research.

From here, retrace your steps back to Main Street which, heading north, becomes Court Street. A lovely place for refreshment is **All Things Tea**, see ⊗③.

## PILGRIM HALL MUSEUM

Continue north along Court Street and you will soon arrive at the **Pilgrim**

Hall Museum ⓭ (tel: 508-746-1620; www.pilgrimhall.org; Feb–Dec daily 9am–4.30pm; charge) in a handsome Greek Revival building dating from 1824, with a recently opened modern extension. The museum features an extensive collection of memorabilia from the first Pilgrim families, a range of Native American artifacts, and the remains of *Sparrow Hawk*, a sailing ship that was wrecked in 1626.

## TOWN WHARF

From the museum, take the next right down Memorial Drive to arrive back at the Tourist Information Center *(see margin, p.89)*. Across the road is the **Town Wharf**, where you could end your Plymouth tour with a seafood meal at the **Lobster Hut**, see ⑪④.

## PLIMOTH PLANTATION

If you have time, it is certainly worth making a visit to **Plimoth Plantation** (137 Warren Avenue; tel: 508-746-1622; www.plimoth.org; Apr–Nov daily 9am–5pm; charge), where the year is always 1627 (they use the 17th-century phonetic spelling for Plymouth, as Governor William Bradford did in his diary). From the Town Wharf, follow Water Street southeast then Sandwich Street for about 2km (1¼ miles) to reach the correct turn-off.

In the plantation's English Village actor-guides dressed in authentic 17th-century costumes and speaking in old English dialects assume the roles of specific historical residents of the colony.

Ask Mistress Alden or Captain Standish about such 18th- or 19th-century figures as Paul Revere or George Washington and they will look at you with incomprehension. The guides do not simply stand around waiting for questions, but go about their 1627 work – salting fish, shearing sheep, baking bread in clay ovens, and even playing ninepins. Even the livestock has been painstakingly 'back-bred' to approximate 17th-century barnyard beasts.

### Wampanoag Homesite

Another part of the plantation is the Wampanoag Homesite, which portrays how Native Americans lived in Massachusetts in the 1620s. The Wampanoag – in their language, 'People of the Dawn' – were a seasonally nomadic tribe, hunting inland in fall and winter, and moving to the coast in spring and summer where they fished and grew corn, squash, and beans. It is a rare opportunity to meet native people in traditional dress and find out about their ancient culture and skills.

**Above from far left:** statue of Massasoit, the Wampanoag chief, on Cole's Hill; Wampanoag dress; pilgrim at Plimoth Plantation; 1627 English Village in the plantation.

**Place to stay**
Next to the Mayflower Society House is Whitfield House (26 North Street; tel: 508-747-6735; www. whitfieldhouse.com), dating from 1782. Fireplaces, antique furniture, and three canopy beds in three of its four bedrooms set an appropriate historical tone at this charming B&B.

## First landfall

Despite all the fuss made over Plymouth Rock, history relates that Plymouth was not the Pilgrim Fathers' first landfall in the New World. That honor belongs to Provincetown *(see p.92)*, at the tip of Cape Cod, where a small party landed on November 21, 1620. The group explored Cape Cod by boat, until they discovered Plymouth, which offered a good harbour, high ground on which they could take defensive positions if attacked, fresh water, and fields cleared and abandoned by Native Americans.

# PROVINCETOWN

*First came the Pilgrim Fathers, later whalers and fishermen, followed by artists, and, most recently, the gay and lesbian community. Now everyone heads to Provincetown, at the hooked tip of Cape Cod, to enjoy its laid-back atmosphere and fantastic national park-protected dunes and beaches.*

---

**DISTANCE** 115 miles (186km) from Boston to P-town by road; 57 miles (92km) by ferry

**TIME** A full day

**START/END** Provincetown's MacMillan Wharf

**POINTS TO NOTE**

The fastest way to Provincetown is by ferry *(see below right)*. If driving, head south out of Boston along Route 1-93, then Route 3, cross the Sagamore Bridge, then follow Route 6, which runs for 60 miles (100km), down the hooked spine of Cape Cod to Provincetown. More scenic is traveling part of the way on Route 6a, running parallel to Route 6 to the west, and passing through several of the Cape's prettiest villages, such as Sandwich and Barnstable. Provincetown is a seasonal destination; many places are closed during much of December and March and all of January and February.

---

Thick with craft shops, art galleries, stores selling nick-nacks and antiques, cafés, restaurants, and bars, 'P-town' is an unashamed tourist destination, but also, thanks to strict town ordinances, a beautiful-looking one. It is no surprise to find that generations of artists have been drawn to P-town and continue to practice here.

An hour-and-a-half ferry ride from Boston (or a two-hour drive), it is possible to make Provincetown a daytrip, although it is far better experienced on an overnight stay. Hiring a bicycle is recommended as distances from one end of P-town to the other are long; try Arnold's (tel: 508-487-0844), just to the left as you leave MacMillan Wharf at 329 Commercial Street, or Ptown Bikes (tel: 508-487-8735; www.ptownbikes.com) at 42 Bradford Street.

## FERRY FROM BOSTON

The following tour assumes you will arrive in P-town by ferry. Running between May and October, there are several fast ferries daily (90 minutes; $79 round trip), with little to choose between the services of **Boston Harbor Cruises** (tel: 617-227-4321; www.bostonharborcruises.com), departing

---

**Tourist information**

Maps and other tourist information are available at the Chamber of Commerce (tel: 508-487-3424; ptownchamber.com; Jan–Mar Mon and Fri 11am–3pm, Apr–May and Nov–Dec Mon–Sat 10.30am–5pm, June–Oct daily 9am–6.30pm), on the right as you leave Mac-Millan Wharf. See also www.province town.com.

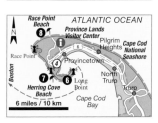

from Long Wharf, near the New England Aquarium *(see p.74)*, and **Bay State Cruise Company** (tel: 877-783-3779; www.baystatecruisecompany.com), departing from the World Trade Center on Seaport Boulevard.

## *MacMillan Wharf*

Ferries dock at **MacMillan Wharf**, toward the end of which you will find the **Expedition Whydah** ❶ (tel: 508-487-8899; whydah.com; charge), a small museum documenting the remains of the pirate ship *Whydah*, which sank in 1717 off the coast of the Cape. Continue down the wharf, past the many boats offering whale watching and other ocean-going tours, to the Chamber of Commerce office for tourist information *(see margin, left)*. Immediately ahead is Commercial Street, P-town's principal retail thoroughfare.

## PILGRIM MONUMENT

Approaching P-town from land or sea, you cannot miss the slender granite tower rising up 252ft 7¹/₂in (77m) from High Pole Hill. To reach the **Pilgrim Monument and Provincetown Museum** ❷ (tel: 508-487-1310; www.pilgrim-monument.org; daily Apr–May and mid-Sept–Nov 9am–5pm, June–mid-Sept 9am–7pm; charge), walk inland from Commercial to Bradford Street, then hike up High Poll Hill Road.

Inspired by the Torre del Mangia in Siena and completed in 1910, the monument commemorates the Pilgrims'

stop in Provincetown in 1620 for six weeks before they moved on to Plymouth *(see p.88)*. To get your bearings of P-town's confusing geography, and for a grand 360-degree view of the Lower Cape, it is worth slogging up the tower's 116 steps and 60 ramps. The fascinating museum at the monument's base is strong on local history, and includes a section on the Arctic explorations of townsman Donald MacMillan (1874–1970).

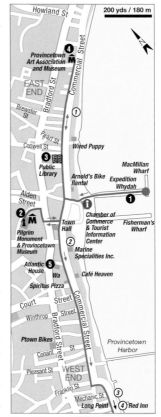

Above from far left: P-town and the Pilgrim Monument behind; typical architecture; browsing the artwork in the Provincetown Art Association and Museum.

**Places to stay**
P-town is packed with guesthouses and holiday rentals. Reserve well in advance for the peak July–Aug season. Rates drop substantially out of season. A fine budget option is Provincetown Inn (1 Commerical Street; tel: 508-487-9500; www.provincetowninn.com), a motel-style resort bounded by water on three sides and with its own pool and direct access to the beach. More upmarket, and inland, is The Brass Key (67 Bradford Street; tel: 1800-842-9858; www.brasskey.com), also with a small pool and spa.

**Provincetown
trolley**
Usually running
between late May
and October, the
Provincetown Trolley
(tel: 508-487-9483)
offers a narrated
sightseeing tour along
Commercial Street
and through the Cape
Cod National Sea-
shore. You can hop
on and off the 40-
minute tour along the
way. Tours depart
from the Town Hall
on Commercial
Street every half-hour
daily between 10am
and 4pm.

## THE EAST END

Return to Commercial Street and head
left toward the **East End**. This is the
artistic end of P-town, packed with
galleries; you will find a concentration
around **The Mews**, see ⑪①. Before
reaching there, pop into the **Public
Library** ❸ (356 Commercial Street;
tel: 508-487-7094; www.ptownlib.
com; Mon and Fri 10am–5pm, Tue and
Thur noon–8pm, Wed 10am–8pm, Sat
10am–2pm, Sun 1–5pm; free), surely
the only library in the world to house
a full-masted half-size replica of an
Indian Schooner (the *Rose Dorothea*).

### Provincetown Art Association

At no. 379 you can get a caffeine boost
at **Wired Puppy** (tel: 508-487-0017;
www.wiredpuppy.com), then power on
to the **Provincetown Art Association
and Museum** ❹ (PAAM; tel: 508-
487-1750; www.paam.org; May–Sept
Mon–Thur 11am–8pm, Fri 11am–
10pm, Sat–Sun 11am–5pm, Oct–May
Thur–Sun noon–5pm; charge) at no.
460. Top-class exhibitions are staged
here, maintaining a tradition that

started in 1899 with the founding of
the Cape Cod School of Art by
Charles Hawthorne.

## THE WEST END

Return to the center of town and
continue along Commercial Street
toward the **West End**. On the way you
will pass many P-town mainstays, including **Ross's Grill**, see ⑪②, at the
Whaler's Wharf; the surplus store
**Marine Specialties Inc.** at no. 235, an
Ali Baba's cave of sale items; the historic
**Atlantic House** ❺ (4 Masonic Place;
tel: 508-487-3821 www.ahouse.com),
better known as the A-House, once
home to the playwright Eugene O'Neill
and now an eternally popular gay bar;
the interior-design store **Wa** (tel: 508-
487-6844; www.waharmony.com), at
no. 220, which has a lovely oriental-
style garden to the rear; **Café Heaven**
(tel: 508-487-9639) at no. 207, a great
place for breakfast or lunch; and, at no.
190, **Spiritus Pizza** (tel: 508-487-2808
www.spirituspizza.com), the place
where everyone heads at 1am once the
town's clubs have shut.

**Right:** classic Cape
Cod detail.

## Coastal cottages

Further down Commercial Street there are a few antiques stores, but once you have followed the road left around the Coast Guard Station the shops are replaced by guesthouses and private residences, with the sole restaurant being **Sal's Place**, see ③. The numerous weatherboard cottages surrounded by flowergardens here are a sight to behold, particularly in the crisp ocean light. Particularly picturesque is the aptly named **Red Inn**, see ❶④, on whose lawns you will often see art classes being held.

### CAPE COD NATIONAL SEASHORE

There are pleasant beaches either side of MacMillan Wharf, but P-town's best strips of sand are part of the **Cape Cod National Seashore (CCNS)**, including **Long Point ❻**, the slender sandbar that hooks back into Cape Cod Bay. You can reach here by walking across the breakwater at the far western end of Commercial Street; the uneven stones can make the crossing a challenge. Once on Long Point you can aim either right to the lighthouse at Wood End or left to the lighthouse on the tip of the sandbar – going in this direction you will pass the P-town nudist beach.

### Along the coast

If you are on a bicycle or in a car, consider exploring more of the beaches and dunes. Heading north along the coast toward the Atlantic side of the Cape, **Herring Cove Beach ❼** is popular with families and a fine spot to watch sunsets. Further around, and pinpointed by another lighthouse, is **Race Point Beach ❽**, behind which is P-town's airport. You will get a fine view of the area from the observation deck above the **Province Lands Visitor Center** (tel: 508-487-1256; www.nps.gov/caco; daily May–Oct 9am–5pm; free), where can find out about ranger-led walks around the national park. Note if you bring your car or bike into the national park area there is a small charge.

If you came by ferry, head back to Macmillan Wharf to return to Boston.

**Long Point homes**
For the first half of the 19th century Long Point was home to a fishing community of 38 houses. As the fishing around here dried up, the homes were put on rafts and floated across to P-town, where many of them still stand, marked by blue-and-white enamel plaques.

# DIRECTORY

A user-friendly alphabetical listing of practical information, plus hand-picked hotels and restaurants, clearly organized by area, to suit all budgets and tastes.

# A

## ADMISSION FEES

**Go Boston Card**: tel: 1-800-887-9103; www.smartdestinations.com. This three, five- or seven-day visitor pass offers admission to over 71 attractions and tours in and around Boston, including several popular sightseeing tours and museums. Cards can be bought online or at the Bostix booths at Faneuil Hall and Copley Square *(see margin, p.19)*, and the Boston Common and Prudential Center visitor information centers *(see p.103)*.

**Boston CityPass**: tel: 1-888-330-5008; www.citypass.com. This gives admission to five sites (Prudential Center Skywalk, Museum of Fine Arts, Museum of Science, New England Aquarium, and Harvard Museum of Natural History or John F. Kennedy Presidential Library & Museum), as well as discounts at several other attractions and restaurants ($46 adults; $29 youths). It is good for nine consecutive days, and is sold online and at all the above locations.

# B

## BUSINESS HOURS

Most **offices** are open Monday to Friday 9am to 5pm. Federal and local government offices are usually open weekdays 8.30am to 4.30pm. **Banks** are open weekdays 9am to 4pm. Some are also open on Thursday until 5pm and Saturday 9am to noon.

# C

## CLIMATE

Boston has four distinct seasons. The first snow generally falls in November and continues intermittently through March. Spring, which can be fleeting, starts in April, and is characterized by crisp, clear days and chilly evenings. June to September can be very hot and humid, although most of the summer is pleasant due to the ocean breeze. Fall is glorious, and the famous New England multicolored foliage peaks in mid-October as the temperature starts to plummet.

For daily weather updates check online at www.accuweather.com.

## CONSULATES

Most embassies are based in Washington, DC, but many countries have consulates in Boston. A complete list can be found at www.state.gov/s/cpr/rls/dpl/32122.htm.

**Canada**: 3 Copley Place, Suite 400; tel: 617-262-247-5190; www.canadainternational.gc.ca/boston.
**Ireland**: 535 Boylston Street; tel: 617-267-9330; www.consulategeneralofirelandboston.org.
**Israel**: 20 Park Plaza; tel: 617-535-0200; boston.mfa.gov.il.
**United Kingdom**: One Broadway, Cambridge; tel: 617-245-4500; ukinusa.fco.gov.uk/en/about-us/other-locations/boston.

## CRIME AND SAFETY

Boston is one of the safest cities in the US, but visitors should always be vigilant. Areas where crime is a problem, such as Dorchester, Mattapan, and Roxbury, offer few tourist attractions, and are on the fringes of the city. One central area to avoid, especially at night, is south of Washington Street and west of Massachusetts Avenue. Avoid the Fenway Victory Gardens in Back Bay Fens, as violent attacks have been reported here.

## CUSTOMS

Anyone over the age of 21 may bring 200 cigarettes, 50 cigars, or 3lbs of tobacco, one liter of alcohol, and a maximum of $100 worth of duty-free gifts. Importing meat products, seeds, plants, or fruits is illegal, as are narcotics. The US permits you to take out anything you wish, but consult with the authorities of your destination country to learn of its customs regulations on entry.

## D

## DISABLED TRAVELERS

Boston caters well to the disabled traveler, with accessible bathrooms and ramps on public buildings, curbsides, and at most attractions. However, it is also an old city with colonial buildings and cobblestone sidewalks, so despite best efforts it is not always perfect. Check the Massachusetts Bay Transit Authority's website (www.

mbta.com) for public transport access information for disabled travelers, including details of its The Ride service for door-to-door paratransit. For more information call 1-888-844-0355, Mon–Fri 7am–11pm, Sat and Sun 8am–5pm. Boston's Commission for Persons with Disabilities can be reached on tel: 617-635-3682 or via www.cityofboston.gov/disability.

## E

## ELECTRICITY

The US uses 110–120V, 60-cycle AC voltage (as opposed to the 220–240V, 50-cycle of Europe). Laptops and many travel appliances are dual voltage and will work, but check first. An adapter will be needed for US sockets.

## EMERGENCY NUMBERS

Ambulance, Fire, and Police: tel: 911.

## G

## GAY TRAVELERS

Massachusetts is famous as the first US state to legalize same-sex marriage. In general Boston is a very integrated city, so you will find gays and straights mingling in many city neighborhoods. The South End has the highest concentration of gay bars *(see p.123 for recommendations)*, and is also the home of the annual Boston Pride parade (www.bostonpride.org) that culminates in a huge carnival.

Above from far left: lazy afternoon on the bank of the Charles River; motorbike cop.

Somerville and Jamaica Plain are popular areas for lesbians to hang out.

The **Greater Boston Business Council** (www.gbbc.org) is the city's gay chamber of commerce, with information on businesses owned, operated, or supported by the local gay community.

# H

## HEALTH AND MEDICAL CARE

Foreign visitors needing medical attention can face stiff bills for one night in a hospital in a semi-private room. It is advisable to arrange med-ical insurance before leaving home.

### *Emergency dental care*
**Tufts Dental School**, 1 Kneeland Street; tel: 617-636-6828; dental. tufts.edu; Mon–Fri 9am–4pm. Emer-gency walk-in clinic with limited admissions.

### *Hospitals*
**Brigham & Women's Hospital**, 75 Francis Street; tel: 617-732-5500; www.brighamandwomens.org.
**Mount Auburn Hospital**, 330 Mount Auburn Street; tel: 617-492-3500; www.mountauburnhospital.org.
**Massachusetts General Hospital**, 55 Fruit Street; tel: 617-726-2000; www. massgeneral.org.
**Tufts Medical Center**, 800 Wash-ington Street; tel: 617-636-5000; www.tuftsmedicalcenter.org.

### *Medical hotlines*
**Beth Israel Deaconess Hospital**, tel: 617-667-7000; www.bidmc.har vard.edu.
**Massachusetts Eye and Ear Infirmary**, tel: 617-523-7900; www.masseyeand ear.org.
**Aids hotline**, tel: 1-800-235-2331; Mon–Thur 9am–8pm, Fri 9am–5pm; www.aac.org.

### *Pharmacies*
Several branches of CVS (www.cvs. com) are open 24 hours, including:
**CVS Pharmacy**, 155 Charles Street; tel: 617-227-0437.
**CVS Pharmacy**, 36 White Street, Cambridge; tel: 617-876-5519.

# I

## INTERNET

Wireless internet access is common in cafés and many student-type hangouts. Many places charge a fee for incre-ments of an hour to 24 hours, but you can also find free hotspots (www.wi-fi hotspotlist.com) throughout the city.

**Boston Public Library**, 700 Boylston Street; tel: 617-536-5400; www.bpl. org; Mon–Thur 9am–9pm, Fri–Sat 9am–5pm. Free wireless connections to the Library's internet service in all 28 branches, with direct plug-in ports available in Bates Hall in the Cen-tral Library.

**Cambridge Public Library**, 359 Broadway, Cambridge; tel: 617-349-

4040; www.cambridgema.gov/cpl.aspx; Mon–Thur 9am–9pm, Fri–Sat 9am–5pm, Sun 1–5pm. Free wireless access in all the branches, with a few internet computer stations available on a first-come-first-served basis for 20-minute or one-hour sessions. Users are allowed up to 15 pages of free printing per day.

## L

## LEGAL MATTERS

In the unfortunate event you are arrested, you are legally allowed to remain silent, and are entitled to free legal representation, provided by the state, if you cannot afford it yourself. You are also entitled to a single phone call. If you do not have family, friends, or a lawyer that can be of assistance, call your embassy or consulate. The legal drinking age in Massachusetts is 21, and driving under the influence is a serious offense that will result in stiff fines and jail time.

## LOST PROPERTY

Most establishments operate their own lost-and-found department, but if you lose something in a public area, go to the local police station to see if it has been handed in.

*Lost or stolen credit cards*
**AMEX**: tel: 1-800-528-4800
**Diners Club/Carte Blanche**: tel: 1-800-234-6377
**MasterCard**: tel: 1-800-627-8372
**Visa**: tel: 1-800-847-2991

## M

## MAPS

Insight Guides' FlexiMap Boston is laminated for durability and easy folding, and contains travel information as well as exceptionally clear cartography. Rubel BikeMaps (www.bikemaps.com) produces great cycling maps for routes in and around Boston.

## MEDIA

**Newspapers**: The city has two daily newspapers: the broadsheet *Boston Globe* (www.boston.com). The *Christian Science Monitor* (www.csmonitor.com), a prestigious online newspaper (Mon–Fri) and weekly print magazine, is published in Boston and is strong on international news.

Free weekly papers include *The Phoenix* (thephoenix.com) and *Weekly Dig* (digboston.com). Both offer good features, well-written arts and music sections, and full city events listings. There is also the *Improper Bostonian* (www.improper.com), a free weekly lifestyle magazine, and the free bimonthly *Stuff* (www.stuffboston.com). All of these are distributed from sidewalk dispensers.

In shops you can buy *Boston Magazine* (www.bostonmagazine.com), a slick, informative monthly magazine with local features and interviews. **Out of Town News** (tel: 617-354-7777) is a kiosk in the middle of Harvard Square that sells a range of national and international publications.

**Radio**: Stations include WBZ (boston.cbslocal.com) on 1030AM for news; WRKO (www.wrko.com) on 680AM for talk; WCRB (www.wcrb.com) on 100.7FM for classical music; WBCN (www.wbcn.com) on 104.1FM for rock music; and WGBH (www.wgbh.org) public radio on 89.7FM for national programs and 99.5FM for classical music.

**Television**: Stations include Channel 2 (www.wgbh.org) for public television; and the national networks CBS on Channel 4 WBZ (boston.cbslocal.com), ABC on Channel 5 WCVB (www.thebostonchannel.com), NBC on Channel 7 WHDH (www1.whdh.com), and Fox on Channel 25 WFXT (www.myfoxboston.com).

## MONEY

Major credit and debit cards are widely accepted. Some smaller restaurants accept cash only; they will usually post it in the menu, or you can check with your waiter beforehand. Car rental agencies and some hotels will require you to have a credit card. ATMs are plentiful.

Traveler's checks are easily converted to cash at any bank, but you will need your passport to prove your identity. Foreign currency exchange is not handled by all banks; your best bet for this is to head to a travel services companies.

**Travelex**, 745 Boylston Street, Boston; www.travelex.com.

**Smoking**
Smoking is banned in all indoor public places across the state, including bars, clubs, and restaurants. In some bars there are outdoor areas set aside for smoking; if not, you have to go out on the street.

**American Express Travel**, 1 State Street, Boston; tel: 617-723-8400; 39 J.F. Kennedy Street, Cambridge; tel: 617-868-2600.

# P

## POST

The main Post Office can be found at 25 Dorchester Avenue (behind South Station; tel: 617-654-5302; www.usps.gov; daily 24 hours). There are many branches across the city, most open Mon–Fri 9am–5pm, including at Logan Airport. Stamps are available in vending machines in airports, hotels, stores, bus and train stations, as well as online.

## PUBLIC HOLIDAYS

All government offices, banks, and post offices close on public holidays. Public transportation does not run as often on these days, but most shops, museums, and other attractions will be open.

**Jan 1**: New Year's Day
**Third Mon Jan**: Martin Luther King Day
**Third Mon Feb**: President's Day
**March/April**: Easter Sunday
**Third Mon Apr**: Patriot's Day
**Last Mon May**: Memorial Day
**July 4**: Independence Day
**First Mon Sept**: Labor Day
**Second Mon Oct**: Columbus Day
**Last Thur and Fri Nov**: Thanksgiving
**Dec 25**: Christmas

# T

## TELEPHONES

**Phone numbers**: All telephone numbers have ten digits. The Greater Boston area code, included in the number even when calling within the city, is 617. Surrounding towns use 508 (Plymouth and Provincetown), 781 (Lexington and Concord), and 978 (Salem and Cape Ann). If you are calling outside the local area then a 1 precedes the 10-digit number.

**Calling from abroad**: To dial Boston from the UK: 00 (international code) + 1 (USA) + a 10-digit number. For calls to other countries from Boston dial the international access code (011), then the country code, city code, and local number. Directory assistance is 555-1212 preceded by 1 and the area code you are calling from or inquiring about; so for Boston call 1-617-555-1212.

**Public telephone boxes**: The popularity of cell (mobile) phones means you will find few public telephone booths in Boston. Newer cell handsets from Europe and Asia work in US cities, but reception in suburban and rural areas tends to be spotty. This is improving as the US upgrades its cell infrastructure. Pay-as-you-go SIMs that will work in your phone, depending on the model, can purchased from several outlets throughout the city. Main companies are AT&T (www.att.com), Sprint (www.sprint.com), and Verizon (www.verizon.com).

## TIME ZONES

Boston is on Eastern Standard Time, which is five hours behind Greenwich Mean Time. The US has four time zones, so Boston is three hours ahead of Los Angeles, two hours ahead of Denver and one hour ahead of Chicago.

## TIPPING

Tipping is voluntary, but unlike in Europe service charges are not added to bills. Waiters, taxi drivers, bartenders, etc will expect gratuities, as this supplements their minimum wage pay. Standard is 15 per cent of the bill, with 20 per cent for above-average service and at better restaurants. Doormen, skycabs, and porters receive $1–2 per bag, and chambermaids, $1–2 per night.

## TOURIST INFORMATION

The **Greater Boston Convention and Visitors Bureau** (Two Copley Place; tel: 617-536-4100/1-888-733-2678; www.bostonusa.com) runs two visitor centers:

**Boston Common Visitor Information Center**, 148 Tremont Street; daily 9am–5pm (the booth here marks the start of the Freedom Trail).

**Prudential Visitor Center**, Center Court, Prudential Center, 800 Boylston Street; Mon–Sat 9am–5pm, Sun 1–5pm.

The **Cambridge Office of Tourism** (4 Brattle Street, Cambridge; tel:

**Above from far left**: New Old South Church in silhouette; Fenway Park.

**Toilets**
Public toilets in Boston are scarce. You can find listings for available facilities online (www.universalhub.com/restrooms). The best options are libraries, hotel lobbies, shopping malls or asking politely at a restaurant or café.

1-800-862-5678/617-441-2884; www.cambridge-usa.org; Mon–Sat 9am–5pm) has a booth in the center of Harvard Square (tel: 617-497-1630; Mon–Sat 9am–5pm, Sun 11am–5pm).

**Massachusetts Office of Travel and Tourism,** 10 Park Plaza, Suite 4510; tel: 617-973-8500; www.massvacation.com; Mon–Fri 9am–5pm. Supplies information on Boston and the state.

**Massport International Information Booth**, Logan International Airport (Terminal E); summer noon–8pm; winter noon–6pm.

There are two **National Park Service Visitor Centers** (www.nps.gov/bost), both open daily 9am to 5pm: Charlestown Navy Yard (tel: 617-242-5601); and Faneuil Hall (tel: 617-242-5642).

## TRANSPORTATION

### Arrival by air

Logan Airport (tel: 1-800-235-6426; www.massport.com) has five terminals (A to E). Airlines do not necessarily use the same terminal for domestic and international flights. There are free shuttle buses that are wheelchair-lift-equipped and run between the terminals. In addition, an on-call (tel: 617-561-1770) lift-equipped van serves all Logan Airport's facilities; it can be requested from any Public Information Booth at the arrivals level/baggage claim.

### Airport to city

Logan is only 3 miles (4.8km) from Downtown Boston. **Logan Shuttle** buses (www.massport.com) connect the terminals' arrival levels with the MBTA Blue Line (T-stop: Airport; tel: 617-222-3200; www.mbta.com). It takes about 10 minutes to Downtown, where you can transfer to the Green Line (T-stop: Government Center) and Orange Line (T-stop: State Street).

The **Silver Line** is a rapid-transit bus service, also part of the MBTA system, which stops at all the airport terminals and connects with the Red Line and Amtrak train (T-stop: South Station), before continuing to the South End.

**Taxis** are stationed outside each terminal. Fares to the city or to Cambridge are approximately $25 (excluding tip and surcharges) providing there are no major traffic jams. A surcharge that covers the tolls ($5.25) and airport fees ($2.25) is added to any trips going into the city. Also see the Massport website for details of flat fares to suburban areas.

**Water shuttles** are a delightful way to approach the city, and convenient if you are staying in Downtown, North End, or the Waterfront. Operators include:

**City Water Taxi** (tel: 617-422-0392; www.citywatertaxi.com; Apr–Dec Mon–Sat 7am–10pm, Sun 7am–8pm, Jan–Mar daily 7am–7pm; $10 one-way, $17 round trip). Private service to around 30 landings in Boston Harbor.

**Rowes Wharf Water Transport** (tel: 617-406-8584; www.roweswharfwater

transport.com; Nov–Apr daily 7am–7pm, April–Nov until 10pm; $10 one-way, $17 round trip). Private service to 30 locations in the harbor.

*Arrival by land*

**By rail**: South Station (Atlantic Avenue and Summer Street) is the east coast terminus for Amtrak (tel: 1-800-872-7245/1, TDD/TTY 1-800-523-6590; www.amtrak.com). Passengers can travel on northbound trains from Washington, DC, New York, and Philadelphia, with connections from all points in the nationwide Amtrak system. In addition, daily trains arrive from Chicago to Boston by way of Cleveland, Buffalo, Rochester, and Albany NY. Prior to arriving at South Station, the train stops at Back Bay Station (145 Dartmouth Street; tel: 617-345-7958), which is convenient for access to Back Bay and the South End.

**By bus**: Several intercity bus companies serve Boston. The two largest, **Greyhound** (tel: 1-800-231-2222; www.greyhound.com) and **Peter Pan** (tel: 1-800-343-9999; www.peterpanbus.com), have daily services to almost anywhere in the US. Greyhound offers a North America Discovery Pass for unlimited travel 7, 15, 30 and 60 days, starting in either the US or Canada and allowing travel to any of their destinations. Services to Cape Cod are provided by **Plymouth & Brockton** (tel: 508-746-0378; www.p-b.com). All buses leave from the bus terminal next to South Station.

**By car**: Free up-to-date traffic information is available from SmartTraveler (www.smarttraveler.com) by dialing 511 on your cell phone.

**From the west**: the Massachusetts Turnpike (Mass Pike or I-90) toll road is the best route into town from the west. Take Exit 18 Cambridge/Allston for Cambridge and Harvard Square; Exit 22 Prudential Center/Copley Square for Back Bay, Fenway, Kenmore Square, and Boston Common; Exit 24 for Downtown and access to Route 93.

**From the south**: Routes 95, 24 and 3 all feed into Route 1 which turns into Route 93 North; Exit 20 (South Station/I-90) is best for Downtown; Exit 23 (Government Center) for Waterfront, and Exit 26 (Storrow Drive) is best for Beacon Hill and Back Bay.

**From the north**: Routes 95, 1 and 93 enter Boston on elevated highway structures; Exit 26 (Storrow Drive) is best for Beacon Hill and Back Bay; Exit 23B-A (Government Center) is best for North End and Downtown; 20B-A (South Station) is best for Waterfront.

*Transportation within Boston*

**Subway**: MBTA (tel: 617-222-3200/1-800-392-6100; www.mbta.com; Mon–Sat 5am–1am, Sun 5.40am–1am) operates the oldest subway in the US. Carriages can get crowded during the rush hours, but it is generally efficient and user-friendly. The four main lines – Red, Green, Orange, and Blue – radiate out from Downtown where the lines intersect; riders can transfer between the lines at no charge. Two Silver Line routes are shown on subway

Above from far left: Leonard P. Zakim Bunker Hill Bridge; travelling on the T; Logan Airport.

maps, but these are both bus services and charge bus rather than subway fares.

If you need transfer to a bus (also run by the MBTA) you can ask for a transfer at the ticket booth. 'Inbound' means toward Downtown – Park Street, Downtown Crossing, State Street, and Government Center. 'Outbound' means away from Downtown. All four lines have branches that extend beyond central Boston. Check the destination on the front of the trains. Last trains leave Downtown around 12.45am; there are minor differences in the last trains between the lines, so check postings in the station.

To use the subway purchase a Charlie Ticket ($2) from a station machine. A single ticket permits travel on the entire 'Outbound' length of a line, but there is an 'Inbound' surcharge on extensions of the Green Line. If you board the T at surface stations where there is no ticket machine, you will need the exact fare, as conductors do not carry change. The **Charlie Card** (www.mbta.com/fares_and_passes/charlie) is a plastic stored-value card. If you use this then each ride is $1.70, and you can get free transfers to MBTA buses (not possible with the Charlie Tickets). Accompanied children under 11 travel free.

**Buses**: Few of MBTA's 160-plus bus routes enter Downtown, and most of these are express services from outlying areas. Route 1 travels along Massachusetts Avenue (from Back Bay) across the Charles River to MIT and on to Harvard Square. Single rides are $1.50 or $1.25 using a Charlie Card. Express buses are $2.80–5. Transfers to the subway are discounted only if you are using a Charlie Card. If you do not have the exact fare you will be given change in the form of a Charlie Ticket.

**Commuter Rail**: The MCTA Commuter Rail (tel: 1-800-392-6100) extends from downtown Boston to as far as 60 miles (almost 100km) away, serving such tourist destinations as Concord and Salem. Trains to the north and the northwest of Boston depart from North Station (135 Causeway Street), while trains to points south and west leave from South Station (Atlantic Avenue and Summer Street). Most south-side commuter trains also stop at Back Bay Station.

**Taxis**: Boston has plenty of taxis, although on a rainy day this seems barely credible. There are also taxi lines at most hotels and highly trafficked areas. Note that Boston taxis are not allowed to pick up in Cambridge and vice versa. All tolls are paid for by the passenger, and there is no charge for extra passengers, but the driver may add a charge for heavy suitcases. For trips over 12 miles (20km) from Downtown there are flat rates.

The following taxi companies take phone bookings:

*Boston:*

**Boston Cab**, tel: 617-536-5010; www.bostoncab.us

**Metro Cab**, tel: 617-782-5500; boston-cab.com

**Town Taxi**, tel: 617-536-5000 www.towntaxiboston.com

Above from far
left: Boston skyline
at night; trolleys are
a quick way of get-
ting to know the city
*(see p.26)*; sailing.

*Cambridge:*
**Cambridge Checker Cab**, tel: 617-497-1500 www.checkercabcambridge.com

### Driving and car rental

Drivers must be aged 21 or above to rent, and rates may be higher if you are under 25. Child seats are available for an additional cost and are compulsory for children under five or under 40lbs (18kg). The speed limit on Interstate highways is 55–65mph (88–104kmh); in the city and surrounding communities it is 20–30mph (35–45kmh). Right turns at a red traffic signal are permitted unless there is a NO TURN ON RED sign. On entering a roundabout (rotary), you must yield to vehicles already in it.

All the major car rental companies have outlets at the airport.

**Avis**, tel: 1-800-331-1212; www.avis.com

**Budget**, tel: 1-800-527-0700; www.budget.com

**Dollar Rent A Car**, tel: 617-634-0006; www.dollar.com

**Enterprise**, tel: 1-800-261-7331; www.enterprise.com

**Hertz**, tel: 1-800-654-3131; www.hertz.com

**National**, tel: 1-877-222-9085; www.nationalcar.com

**Thrifty**, tel: 1-877-283-0898: www.thrifty.com

### Bicycle rental

Boston has plenty of dedicated trails that are good for both cyclist and in-line skaters. Hubway (www.thehubway.com) is a new bike sharing system offering 600 bikes at 61 locations across the city; casual membership is possible for 24-hours ($5) or three days ($12), with no extra charges as long as you don't use the bike for more than 30 minutes riding between each docking station. Bikes may be rented from:

**Community Bicycle Supply**, 496 Tremont Street; tel: 617-542-8623; www.communitybicycle.com; Apr–Sept Mon–Fri 10am–7pm, Sat 10am–6pm, Sun noon–5pm, Oct–Mar, Mon–Sat 10am–6pm, Wed and Fri until 7pm.

**Urban Adventours**; 103 Atlantic Avenue; tel: 617-670-0637; www.urbanadventours.com; bike rental (from $35 a day) and tours

## VISAS

Immigration into the US is handled by the US Citizenship and Immigration Service (tel: 1-800-375-5283; www.uscis.gov). Visitors must have a valid passport, visa, or other accepted documentation. The US offers the Visa Waiver Program for those coming on vacation for a maximum of 90 days. With 36 countries participating, the program allows for select travelers to enter the US with only a machine readable passport. Recent increased security now requires all VWP participants to apply with the Electronic System for Travel Authorization online. This is quick to do and can occur at any point before entry into the US. The rules are continually evolving, so check USCIS before you set off (tel: 202-663-1225; www.travel.state.gov/visa/index.html).

## Boston Common and Downtown

### Ames

1 Court Street; tel: 617-979-8120; www.ameshotel.com; T-stop: State; $$$

The 114 rooms at this super-hip hotel are decorated in minimalist grey and white, a contrast with the exterior decorative flourishes of this lovely 1893 building. In-house restaurant Woodward is an appealing, contemporary styled tavern.

### The Langham

250 Franklin Street; tel: 617-451-1900; boston.langhamhotels.com/index.html; T-stop: State; $$$$

Based in the historic landmark that was once the Federal Reserve Bank. Rooms are decorated to reflect the building's opulent history, and it has all the amenities you would expect. Its Café Fleuri offers a brasserie-style menu, and is best-known for its Saturday chocolate bar buffet and elaborate Sunday brunch.

### Nine Zero

90 Tremont Street; tel: 617-772-5800; www.ninezero.com; T-stop: Park Street; $$$$

One of Boston's sleekest boutique hotels, offering high-tech, high-speed, high-touch amenities along with personalized service, custom-designed beds and down comforters. The restaurant serves some of the best steaks in town.

## The North End and Charlestown

### Bulfinch Hotel

107 Merrimac Street; tel: 617-624-0202; www.bulfinchhotel.com; T-stop: North Station or Haymarket; $$$$

Occupying a restored nine-story triangular corner, or flatiron, building, this sophisticated hotel has 80 contemporary-styled, non-smoking rooms and a groovy tapas bar on site.

### The Constitution Inn

150 Third Avenue, Charlestown; tel: 617-241-8400/1-800-495-9622; www.constitutioninn.org; T-stop: Haymarket then bus 93; $$

This former YMCA, located near the USS *Constitution*, offers plainly furnished non-smoking rooms, some with kitchenettes. Rates include access to a state-of-the-art health club with an indoor heated pool, sauna, and weight room.

### Fairmont Battery Wharf

3 Battery Wharf; tel: 617-994-9000/800-441-1414; www.fairmont.com/batterywharf; T-stop: North Station or Haymarket; $$$$

Split across three buildings at the revamped Battery Wharf, this waterside located luxe hotel is handy for the North End and only a short stroll to downtown.

---

Price for a double room for one night without breakfast:

| | |
|---|---|
| $$$$ | over $300 |
| $$$ | $200–300 |
| $$ | $100–200 |
| $ | below $100 |

### Friend Street Hostel

234 Friend Street; tel: 617-934-2413;
www.friendstreethostel.com; T-stop:
North Station or Haymarket; $

Clued-up, friendly owners have made
this new 40-bed hostel (split across
three mixed and two single sex
dorms) in an atmospheric 150-year
old building a top choice for budget
travelers. They've turned the old pub
downstairs into a cool internet café.

### Onyx Hotel

155 Portland Street; tel: 617-557-
9955; www.onyxhotel.com; T-stop:
Haymarket; $$$

The 112 rooms in this boutique hotel
are decorated in a sophisticated palette
of black, taupe, and red, and offer all
the latest high-tech amenities. Their
sleek Ruby Room bar hops at cock-
tail hour. Pet-friendly.

## Harvard

### Charles Hotel

1 Bennett Street, Cambridge;
tel: 617-864-1200; www.charles
hotel.com; T-stop: Harvard; $$$$

The Charles Hotel offers restrained
Shaker-inspired luxury, with incredible
antique quilts gracing the walls, and
impeccable service. All rooms are well
appointed and include high-tech
amenities. The Regattabar is a great
jazz venue, and the Rialto restaurant is
a mainstay of the city's gourmet circuit.

### Hotel Veritas

1 Remington St, Cambridge; tel: 617-
520-5000; www.thehotelveritas.com;
T-stop: Harvard; $$$

Harvard's traditional crimson is ban-
ished from this intimate boutique
hotel that mixes art-deco with contemporary chic. The 31 rooms are on
the small side but come with lovely
beds and linens and specially commissioned art on the walls.

### The Inn at Harvard

1201 Massachusetts Avenue,
Cambridge; tel: 617-491-2222/1-
800-458-5886; www.hotelsinharvard
square.com; T-stop: Harvard; $$

Architect and Harvard grad Graham
Gund designed this four-story hotel,
modeled after the Isabella Stewart
Gardner Museum, to blend in with
the university buildings. The 111
rooms built around a four-story
atrium are delightful and were all
recently renovated.

### Mary Prentiss Inn

6 Prentiss Street, Cambridge;
tel: 617-661-2929; maryprentiss
inn.com; T-stop: Porter; $$$

This historic neoclassical Greek Revival building has 20 rooms with
exposed beams, shutters, and antiques;
some have wood-burning fireplaces
and Jacuzzis. Rates include a full
breakfast and complimentary afternoon tea. There is a lush outdoor deck,
and free parking.

## Charles River and MIT

### Courtyard Boston Cambridge

777 Memorial Drive, Cambridge; tel:
617-492-7777; www.marriott.com/
hotels/travel/boscy-courtyard-

**Above from far
left:** Liberty Hotel,
based in the former
Charles Street Jail
*(see p.111).*

**B&Bs**
Bed and breakfast
accommodations
are not thick on the
ground in Boston,
but those that are
can be of a high
standard. A couple
of agencies to try
are Bed & Breakfast
Agency of Boston
(tel: 617-720-3540
or 800-248-9262;
www.boston-bnb
agency.com) and
Bed and Breakfast
Associates Bay
Colony (tel: 888-
486-6018; www.bnb
boston.com). Prices
typically range from
$100 to $160 for a
double room.

boston-cambridge; T-stop: Central, then bus 47; $$

Conveniently situated on the Cambridge side of the Charles River, equidistant from Harvard and MIT, this Marriot-run hotel's river-facing rooms provide the best-value Boston skyline views.

### Kendall Hotel

350 Main Street, Cambridge; tel: 617-577-1300; kendall hotel.com; T-stop: Kendall/MIT; $$$$

A boutique hotel in a beautifully renovated 1893 Victorian firehouse, with 73 rooms and four suites; those in the seven-story tower have Jacuzzi baths with separate showers. It is located in the heart of Kendall Square next to MIT.

### Le Meridien Cambridge

20 Sidney Street, Cambridge; tel: 617-577-0200; www.hotelatmit. com; T-stop: Central; $$$

As you would expect at a hotel owned by MIT (but managed by Starwood), the rooms here are big on gadgets, with Sony Playstations, dataports, and ergonomically designed furniture. The art is from the MIT collection and the DeCordova Museum in Lincoln *(see*

*p.87)*. There is a peaceful rooftop garden, and the hotel is convenient for Central Square's restaurant and nightlife scene.

### Royal Sonesta

40 Edwin Land Boulevard, Cambridge; tel: 617-806-4200; www.sonesta.com/Boston; T-stop: Lechmere; $$$

Many of the Sonesta's 400 rooms offer great views across the Charles River. There are plenty of facilities, and the hotel is close to the Science Museum, CambridgeSide Galleria, and Kendall Square. Its restaurant Dante serves award-winning Italian fare.

### Beacon Hill

### Beacon Hill Hotel

25 Charles Street; tel: 617-723-7575; www.beaconhillhotel.com; T-stop: Charles/MGH; $$$

Just steps from Boston Common, this small hotel in a converted 1830s townhouse has 12 traditionally furnished rooms, all with flat-screen TVs and abundant amenities. It is also home to the popular Beacon Hill Bistro *(see p.116)*.

### John Jeffries House

14 David G. Mugar Way; tel: 617-367-1866; www.johnjeffrieshouse.com; T-stop: Charles/MGH; $$

An old-world air hangs in this elegant, comfortable 46-room inn. Accommodation options range from studios to deluxe units for up to three people, most with kitchenettes.

| Price for a double room for one night without breakfast: | |
|---|---|
| $$$$ | over $300 |
| $$$ | $200–300 |
| $$ | $100–200 |
| $ | below $100 |

## Liberty Hotel

215 Charles Street; tel: 617-224-4000; www.libertyhotel.com; T-stop: Charles/MGH; $$$$

The former Charles Street Jail (built in 1851) has been inventively renovated so that each of the 300 rooms integrate the building's history with a crisp, modern aesthetic. Original prison catwalks linking public spaces and magnificent soaring windows have been preserved. The pick of its restaurants is Lydia Shire's Scampo.

## XV Beacon

15 Beacon Street; tel: 617-670-1500; www.xvbeacon.com; T-stop: Park St; $$$$

This boutique hotel combines classic opulence with high design. All 62 rooms in the 1903 beaux arts building have gas fireplaces, 4-poster beds, CD players, and heated towel racks.

### Back Bay

## 463 Beacon Street Guest House

463 Beacon Street; tel: 617-536-1302; www.463beacon.com; T-stop: Hynes; $$

This turn-of-the-20th-century brownstone has 19 comfortable and affordable rooms with private baths, phones, and TVs. There are also four apartments with kitchenettes, if you need more room or want a longer stay.

## Back Bay Hotel

350 Stuart Street, Back Bay; tel: 617-266 7200; www.doylecollection.com; T-stop: Arlington; $$$

Located in the former Boston Police Headquarters, this popular hotel offers well-appointed rooms with Wi-Fi, multi-head showers, down-filled comforters, and other luxury amenities.

## Colonnade Hotel

120 Huntington Avenue; tel: 617-424-7000; www.colonnadehotel.com; T-stop: Copley; $$$$

A $25 million renovation upgraded the Colonnade to sleek and modern. The rooms have a distinct European feel with blonde woods, chrome, and earth tones. Their rooftop pool, 11 stories above the city, is the only one in Boston.

## The Eliot Hotel

370 Commonwealth Avenue; tel: 617-267-1607; www.eliothotel.com; T-stop: Hynes; $$$

Promising a 'touch of Paris in Boston' this elegant boutique option has 95 rooms and suites. Also here is Clio, one of the city's finest restaurants.

## Newbury Guest House

261 Newbury Street; tel: 617-437-7668; www.newburyguesthouse.com; T-stop: Hynes; $$

Three 1880s single-family Victorian homes were renovated in the 1990s to create this elegant 32-room inn. The rooms retain some of the 19th-century decorative details. There are quieter rooms in the back. Breakfast included.

## The Taj Boston

15 Arlington Street; tel: 617-536-5700/800-241-3333; www.tajhotels.com; T-stop: Arlington; $$$

**Above from far left:** XV Beacon boutique hotel; Liberty Hotel.

Some of the rooms and suites at this elegant hotel overlook the Public Garden. If you are lucky enough to have a real fireplace, you can ring the Fireplace Butler, who will offer you a menu of different woods to burn.

### The Beech Tree Inn
83 Longwood Avenue, Brookline; tel: 617-277-1620; www.thebeech treeinn.com; T-stop: Longwood; $$

This B&B is bit of a hike west of the Fenway, in a turn-of-the-century Victorian home. Each of its 10 rooms is furnished with books and a fireplace. Breakfast is included, and there is a pleasant backyard patio.

### Boston International Youth Hostel
12 Hemenway Street; tel: 617-536-9455; www.bostonhostel.org; T-stop: Hynes; $

Year-round budget accommodations in dorms (single-sex and co-ed) and private double rooms, all with shared baths. Non YH-members are accepted, and rates include breakfast. There are kitchen and laundry facilities.

### Hotel Commonwealth
500 Commonwealth Avenue; tel: 617-933-5000; www.hotelcommon wealth.com; T-stop: Kenmore; $$$$

In a location that is very handy for Fenway Park, this 149-room hotel is also home to the busy brasserie Eastern Standard *(see p.118)*. Rooms feature free Wi-Fi and marble bathrooms.

### Best Western Plus – The Inn at Longwood
342 Longwood Avenue; tel: 617-731-4700; www.innatlongwood. com; T-stop: Green Line D Train to Longwood; $

161 nicely furnished and fully equipped rooms in the heart of Longwood Medical Area and near Back Bay attractions.

### YMCA of Greater Boston
316 Huntington Avenue, Fenway; tel: 617-536-7800, www.ymcaboston. org; T-stop: Orange Line to Northeastern; $

Affordable clean rooms in a handy location. From mid-August to mid-May it's men-only. Guests have full use of the athletic facilities.

### 40 Berkeley
40 Berkeley Street; tel: 617-375-2524; www.ywcaboston.org/ berkeley; T-stop: Back Bay/South End; $

Dorms and private rooms are appealing at this large, popular hostel that used to be a YMCA. Amenities include a dining room, laundry, movie

| Price for a double room for one night without breakfast: | |
|---|---|
| $$$$ | over $300 |
| $$$ | $200–300 |
| $$ | $100–200 |
| $ | below $100 |

room and lovely courtyard garden. Rates include breakfast.

### Chandler Inn Hotel

26 Chandler Street; tel: 617-482-3450/1-800-842-3450; www.chandlerinn.com; T-stop: Back Bay/South End; $$

Some of the 56 rooms at this gay-friendly hotel are quite small, as are the baths, but they are comfortable and stylish. If you want quiet, request a room several floors up from the rowdy ground-floor sports bar.

### Clarendon Square Inn

198 West Brookline Street; tel: 617-536-2229; www.clarendonsquare.com; T-stop: Back Bay/South End or Symphony; $$

Beautifully appointed, gay-friendly Victorian B&B offering the amenities of a small luxury hotel and the warmth of a small inn. Rooms have wood-burning fireplaces, dataports, and DVD players. The views of the Boston skyline from the rooftop hot tub are fantastic.

## Waterfront and Fort Point Channel

### Boston Harbor Hotel

70 Rowes Wharf; tel: 617-439-7000/800-752-7077; www.bhh.com; T-stop: Aquarium; $$$$

Board the airport water shuttle at Logan and, seven minutes later, step into one of the city's premier waterside hotels. Each of the 230 rooms has either a harbor or skyline view. 18 are designed for the physically disabled. Its restaurant Meritage offers superb dining. Oenophiles should inquire about their annual wine festival.

### Harborside Inn

185 State Street; tel: 617-723-7500; www.harborsideinnboston.com; T-stop: Aquarium; $$

Not actually on the water, but still in a convenient location for the Waterfront. The 98 rooms in this renovated warehouse have high ceilings, exposed brick walls, oriental rugs, and hardwood floors. Quieter rooms face away from State Street.

### Intercontinental Hotel

510 Atlantic Avenue; tel: 617-747-1000/866-493-6495; www.intercontinentalboston.com; T-stop: Aquarium/South Station; $$$$

Luxury hotel well situated between Rowes Wharf, the Children's Museum, South Station, and the Financial District, and an easy subway or water-taxi ride from Logan Airport. Many of its 423 rooms and suites have Waterfront views. Its Miel 'Brasserie Provençale' restaurant serves high-quality French food throughout the day.

### Seaport Boston Hotel

1 Seaport Lane; tel: 617-385-4000; www.seaporthotel.com; T-stop: Seaport World Trade Center; $$$$

This Waterfront hotel has 427 state-of-the-art rooms with hand-crafted cherry furnishings, marble baths, and desks. The luxurious health club includes a 50ft (15m) heated pool and extensive exercise facilities.

**Above from far left:** outside dining area at the Harborside Inn.

# RESTAURANTS

## Gourmet Dumpling House

52 Beach Street; tel: 617-338-6223; www.gourmetdumpling.com; daily 11–2am; T-stop: Chinatown; $

This phenomenally popular (and deservedly so) Chinatown place crams them in for hand-made dumplings and brilliant Chinese food; many swear by their addictively spicey Szechuan-style bubbling whole fish.

## Hong Kong Eatery

79 Harrison Avenue; tel: 617-423-0838; www.hongkongeatery.com; Sun–Thur 11am–10.30pm, Fri and Sat until 11pm; T-stop: Chinatown; $

Tempting bbq pork ribs and full ducks hang in the window at this little restaurant, heavily patronized by local Chinese, which serves excellent food.

## KO Prime

Nine Zero Hotel, 90 Tremont Street; tel: 617-772-0202; www.koprime boston.com; Mon–Fri 6–11am, Sat–Sun 8am–noon, Tue–Fri 6am–10pm, Sat 5.30pm–10pm; T-stop: Park Street; $$$

Chef Ken Oringer's stylish steakhouse, decorated with cow hide, emphasizes farm-fresh produce, including grass-fed Kobe and Wagyu beef, and seafood. The wine list is extensive

## Locke-Ober

3 Winter Place; tel: 617-542-1340; www.lockeober.com; Mon–Fri 5–10pm, Sat 5–11pm; $$$

Women were banned from these historic premises for nearly a century; today, a dress-code is still in operation if you want to dine in the main restaurant, although jeans are allowed at the bar. Many traditional favorites, such as JFK's lobster stew and calf's liver with bacon, remain on the menu from days of old.

## o ya

9 East Street; tel: 617-654-9900; www.oyarestaurantboston.com; Tue–Thur 5–9.30pm, Fri–Sat 5–10pm; T-stop: South Station; $$$$

Inventive gourmet sushi and other Japanese-inspired dishes here will blow your tastebuds away – portions are small and designed to be paired with o ya's excellent sake selection. Start saving up for the incredible 17-course chef's tasting menu.

## Sakurabana

57 Broad Street; tel: 617-542-4311; www.sakurabanaonline.com; Mon–Thur 11.30am–9.30pm, Fri 11.30am–10pm, Sat 5pm–10pm; T-stop: State; $$

This Japanese restaurant may have perfunctory décor, but the lines for lunch are testament to its simple, tasty food, with a few inventive twists.

| Price guide for a three-course dinner for one, excluding beverages, tax, and tip: | |
|---|---|
| $$$$ | $60 and above |
| $$$ | $40–60 |
| $$ | $20–40 |
| $ | $20 and below |

## The North End

### Bricco

241 Hanover Street; tel: 617-248-6800; www.bricco.com; Tue–Sun 11– 2am; T-stop: Haymarket; $$$$

An upscale boutique Italian restaurant preparing regional treats such as handmade pasta. The waiters will urge you to order a 'traditional' meal with several courses, so come prepared with an empty stomach and full wallet.

### Mare

135 Richmond Street; tel: 617-723-6273; www.marenatural.com; daily 5pm–11pm; T-stop: Haymarket; $$$

Offering 'natural coastal Italian' cuisine, Mare's sophisticated, contemporary fit-out sets it apart from the traditional North End trattorias. The seafood is all organic and sustainable and they also have gluten-free pasta.

### Pomodoro

319 Hanover Street; tel: 617-367-4348; Tue–Fri 4–11pm, Sat–Sun 11am–11pm; T-stop: Haymarket; $$

A cozy, casual trattoria serving fresh and tasty dishes based on seasonal local ingredients. Consistent winner of food awards, and favorite among critics and locals. Come early to grab one of the eight tables. Cash only.

## Harvard

### Café Algiers

40 Brattle Street, Cambridge; tel: 617-492-1557; daily 8.30am–10.45pm; T-stop: Harvard; $$

Hang out with Harvard's boho crowd at this atmospherically North African-styled place, serving a reasonably priced menu of well prepared Middle Eastern standards. The falafel has a unique twist and the handmade lamb sausage is seasoned to perfection. Handy for movies at the adjoining repertory theater.

### Casablanca

40 Brattle Street, Cambridge; tel: 617-876-0999; www.casablanca-restaurant.com; Mon–Fri 11.30am–2.30pm, Sun–Wed 6–10pm, Thur–Sat 6–10.30pm; T-stop: Harvard; $$$

In the same complex as Café Algiers, this buzzing and reliable place takes its design cues from the famous movie. A Mediterranean menu with refreshing interpretations of Middle Eastern dishes; tapas available at the bar tables.

### Harvest

44 Brattle Street, Cambridge; tel: 617-868-2255; harvestcambridge.com; Mon–Sat 11.30am– 2pm, Sun–Thur 5.30–10pm, Fri–Sat 5.30–11pm, Sun 11.30am–2.30pm, 5.30–10pm; T-stop: Harvard; $$$

Chef Mary Dumont focuses on the region's freshest seasonal ingredients to prepare dishes interpreted from around the world. The atmosphere is relaxed, but has a distinct business-account feel. It offers dining in one of the few garden terraces around Harvard Square.

### Rialto

Charles Hotel, 1 Bennett Street, Cambridge; tel: 617-661-5050; www.rialto-restaurant.com; Mon–Sat 5.30–10pm, Sun 5.30–9pm; T-stop: Harvard; $$$$

**Above from far left:** seafood is a staple of New England cooking; lunch in the *Cheers* bar in Beacon Hill (84 Beacon Street); upmarket desert; elegant interior of Locke-Ober.

Perennial favorite of gourmands. Chef Jody Adams helms this recently renovated restaurant specializing in regional Italian cuisine with a focus on seafood. Menu changes region and ingredients seasonally. The wine list offers an interesting range from organic and small vineyards.

## Tamarind Bay

75 Winthrop Street, Cambridge; tel: 617-491-4552; www.tamarind-bay. com; Mon–Fri noon–2.30pm, 5–10.30pm, Sat–Sun noon–3pm, 5–10.30pm; T-stop: Harvard; $$$

Far from your standard tandoori and curry joint, Tamarind Bay offers authentic, unusual offerings from the various regions of the Indian subcontinent. The environment is dark and a little more sophisticated than usual too.

## Blue Room

1 Kendall Square Complex, Cambridge; tel: 617-494-9034; www.the blueroom.net; Sun 11am–2.30pm, 5–9pm, Mon–Thur 5–10pm, Fri–Sat 5–11pm; T-stop: Kendall Square (10-minute walk); $$$

Comfortable, casual restaurant serving contemporary innovative and eclectic food basement setting. The service is informal but impeccable, and the wine list always includes interesting selections that pair beautifully with the menu.

## Craigie on Main

853 Main Street, Cambridge; tel: 617-497-5511; www.craigieonmain.com; Tue–Thur 5.30–10pm, Fri–Sat 5.30–

10.30pm, Sun 11am–2pm, 5.30–10pm; T-stop: Central Square; $$$$

Chef Tony Maw's award-winning restaurant, where quality organic and local ingredients dictate the dishes on the menu. Also offers a great Sunday brunch with dishes such as house smoked salmon and bluefish rillettes.

## Helmand Restaurant

143 First Street, Cambridge; tel: 617-492-4646; www.helmandrest aurant.com; Sun–Thur 5–10pm, Fri–Sat 5–11pm; T-stop: Lechmere; $$

A favorite among locals. The food is aromatic, and the flavors are exotic in an area where most of the other restaurants are pretty generic chains catering to shoppers at the nearby CambridgeSide Galleria mall.

## Salts

798 Main Street, Cambridge; tel: 617-876-8444; www.saltsrestaurant. com; Tue–Sat 6–10pm; T-stop: Central Square; $$$$

Small restaurant serving a limited but focused French-inspired American contemporary menu. Their signature duck is cooked to perfection. The cozy, soothingly decorated room makes this a great place for a romantic meal.

Price guide for a three-course dinner for one, excluding beverages, tax, and tip:

| | |
|---|---|
| $$$$ | $60 and above |
| $$$ | $40–60 |
| $$ | $20–40 |
| $ | $20 and below |

## Beacon Hill

### Beacon Hill Bistro

25 Charles Street; tel: 617-723-1133;
www.beaconhillhotel.com; Mon–Fri
7–10am, 11.30am–3pm, 5.30–
11pm, Sat 7.30–10am, 10am–3pm,
5.30–11pm, Sun 7.30–10am,
10am–3pm, 5.30–10pm; T-stop:
Charles/MGH; $$$

French food with a New England in-
fluence in a long, narrow room lined
with leather banquettes and mirrors.
The sophisticated atmosphere makes it
ideal for intimate conversation. Week-
end brunch is popular.

### Bin 26 Enoteca

26 Charles Street; tel: 617-723-5939;
www.bin26.com; Mon–Thur noon–
10pm, Fri noon–11pm, Sat 11am–
11pm, Sun 11am–10pm; T-stop:
Charles/MGH; $$

Not so much a wine bar as a temple
to wine. Collages of bottle labels are
lacquered on the back wall, and 'chan-
deliers' of upside-down bottles cover
the bathroom ceilings. The wine list
has over 60 offerings by the glass. Be
sure to stop the manager for his advice
on pairing the bar's best with the small
and savory dishes.

### Lala Rokh

97 Mount Vernon Street; tel: 617-
720-5511; www.lalarokh.com; Mon–
Fri noon–3pm, 5.30–10pm, Sat–Sun
5.30–10pm; T-stop: Charles/MGH; $$

Sophisticated Persian-inspired cuisine,
with elements of Indian, Turkish, and
Armenian flavors, in a romantically
styled townhouse. The combination of
ingredients brings the Middle Eastern
food to a new level. Vegetarian-friendly.

### No. 9 Park

9 Park Street; tel: 617-742-9991;
www.no9park.com; Mon–Fri 5.30–
10pm; T-stop: Park Street; $$$$

Recognized as one of Boston's top
restaurants, No. 9 Park prepares Euro-
pean country cuisine in a Bulfinch-
designed 19th-century mansion over-
looking the Common. A simpler bar
menu is also available in the bar on a
first-come-first-served basis.

## Back Bay

### Davio's

75 Arlington Street; tel: 617-357-4810;
www.davios.com; Mon–Tue 11.30am–
3pm, 5–10pm, Wed–Fri 11.30am–
3pm, 5–11pm, Sat 5–11pm, Sun
5pm–10pm; T-stop: Arlington; $$$

Based in the historic Paine Furniture
Building, Davio's staying power is testa-
ment to the quality of its service and
food, which is straightforward northern
Italian fare using the finest of ingredients. At lunch there is a takeout counter,
serving sandwiches, salads, and soups.

### Jasper White's Summer Shack

50 Dalton Street; tel: 617-867-9955;
www.summershackrestaurant.com;
Nov–Mar Mon–Fri 5–11pm, Apr–Oct
Sun–Thur 11.30am–10pm, Fri and
Sat 11.30am–11pm; bar until 1am;
T-stop: Hynes; $$

Although the word 'shack' is a bit of
a stretch, few will quibble as they chow
down on pan-roasted lobster, steamers,
and fresh seafood chowder.

**Above from far
left:** Salts prepares
dishes with locally
sourced produce;
peach gnocchi at
the Top of the
Hub *(see p.60)*;
popular local chain;
making fresh pasta
at No. 9 Park.

### Sonsie

327 Newbury Street; tel: 617-351-2500; sonsieboston.com; Mon–Tue 11.30am–2.30pm, 6–11pm, Wed–Fri until midnight, Sat 11.30am–3pm, 6pm–midnight, Sun 11.30am–3pm, 6–11pm; T-stop: Arlington; $$

Indulge in a spot of people-watching from Sonsie's sidewalk tables. Unusual pizza combos, seasonal menus built around a single ingredient and general menu descriptions might seem overly fussy, but the dishes generally work.

### Sorrelina

1 Huntington Avenue; tel: 617-412-4600; www.sorrelinaboston.com; Sun–Thur 5.30–10pm, Fri–Sat 5.30–11pm; T-stop: Arlington; $$

Serving regional Italian dishes with a contemporary twist, this sophisticated restaurant is a fancy occasion place just across from Copely Square. Their bar is a good place for a snack or cocktail.

### Back Bay Fens

### Betty's Wok & Noodle Diner

250 Huntington Avenue; tel: 617-424-1950; www.bettyswokandnoodle.com; Tue–Thur 11am–10pm, Fri–Sat 11.30am–11pm, Sun–Mon 11.30am–9pm; T-stop: Symphony; $$

Price guide for a three-course dinner for one, excluding beverages, tax, and tip:

| | |
|---|---|
| $$$$ | $60 and above |
| $$$ | $40–60 |
| $$ | $20–40 |
| $ | $20 and below |

Casual restaurant featuring an unusual fusion of Asian and Latino cuisines. Noodles are paired with a South American-style citrus sauce, and 'Juantons' are filled with spicy Cuban pork filling. Drinks run from sangria to sake.

### Eastern Standard

528 Commonwealth Avenue; tel: 617-532-9100; www.easternstandard boston.com; Mon–Thur 7.30–10am, 11.30am–2.30pm, 5–11pm, Fri–Sat until midnight, Sun 10.30am–3pm, 5–11pm; T-stop: Kenmore; $$$

Next to the Commonwealth Hotel, the menu at this Parisian-style bistro features everything from veal schnitzel to beef Wellington via the classic *moules et frites*. The wine list is long and well picked, and the creative cocktail menu is a labor of love. Single diners can pull up a seat at its 46ft (14m) -long bar.

### The Mission Bar and Grill

724 Huntington Avenue; tel: 617-566-1244; www.themissionbar.com; daily 11am–midnight; T-stop: Brigham Circle; $$

The mission of this 'gastropub' seems to be beer, with a respectable list of bottled ales and on-tap brews. They also get the food right. French fries are made with sweet potatoes, and salads are garnished with homemade croutons, not drowned in oil.

### Petit Robert Bistro

468 Commonwealth Avenue; tel: 617-375-0699; www.petitrobert bistro.com; daily 11am–11pm; T-stop: Kenmore; $$

Simple French food without fuss or high prices. Chef Jacky Robert's goal is to create a bistro where diners can eat for under $20. Ingredients from the best purveyors create upmarket steak frites, lobster bouillabaisse, and croque monsieur. There is a second branch in the South End at 480 Columbus Avenue (tel: 617-867-0600).

## The South End

### The Butcher Shop
552 Tremont Street; tel: 617-423-4800; thebutchershopboston.com; Sun–Mon 11am–11pm, Tue–Sat 11am–midnight; T-stop: Back Bay; $$$
One of Boston's top chefs, Barbara Lynch, runs this small wine bar and charcuterie. Stop in for a generous pour of Pinot Noir with a small plate of antipasti, before a performance at the Boston Center for the Arts opposite.

### Delux Café
100 Chandler Street; tel: 617-338-5258; Mon–Sat 5pm–11.30pm; T-stop: Back Bay; $$
The quirky decor of old Elvis records on the walls and Cartoon Network on the television screens make Delux a magnet for hipsters. You cannot go wrong with their famous quesadillas or one of their comfort-food specials.

### The Franklin Café
278 Shawmut Avenue; tel: 617-350-0010; www.franklincafe.com; Mon–Sun 5.30–1.30am; T-stop: Back Bay; $$
Delicious bistro-style dishes served in a romantic, darkly lit small space,

tucked away on sleepy Shawmut Avenue. Try the seasonal sides, classic cocktails, and daily gourmet specials.

### Myers+Chang
1145 Washington Avenue; tel: 617-542-5200; www.myersandchang.com; Sun–Wed 11.30am–10pm, Thur–Sat 11.30am–11pm; T-stop: Back Bay; $$$
Engaging, youthful Asian restaurant with a menu of dishes designed for sharing – their hakka eggplant is the best, while their tiger's tears, Thai-style steak is addictively spicey.

## Waterfront and Fort Point Channel

### Menton
354 Congress Street; 617-737-0099; www.mentonboston.com; Sun–Thu 5.30–9.45pm, Fri–Sat 5.30–10pm; T-stop: Courthouse; $$$$
Named after a small French village on the border with Italy, this is Barbara Lynch's latest high-end affair serving either two four-course prix-fixe menus or the chef's seven course tasting menu: an elaborate affair that lasts all evening.

### No-Name
15 Fish Pier (just off Northern Avenue); 617-338-7539; noname restaurant.com; daily 11am–10pm; T-stop: World Trade Center; $
The antithesis of a tourist trap, No-Name serves no-frills seafood for reasonable prices in a large dining room simply decorated with blown-up photos of Boston's past. Preparations are simple, but the chowder has a reputation.

**Above from far left:** wash it down with Sam Adams; simple plates of seafood at No-Name; sweet potato fries.

### 21st Amendment

150 Bowdoin Street; tel: 617-227-7100; www.21stboston.com; daily; T-stop: Park Street

The 21st Amendment repealed Prohibition, and the lawyers, law students, legislators, and Beacon Hill locals congregating in this cozy dark pub with pews still enjoy that right.

### 28 Degrees

1 Appleton Street; 617-728-0728; www.28degrees-boston.com; daily; T-stop: Arlington

Named after the optimum chilling temperature for Martinis, this chic bar and restaurant offers soft lighting, comfortable banquettes, and a stylish clientele.

### 49 Social

49 Temple Place; 617-45101416; www.49social.com; daily; T-stop: Park Street/Downtown Crossing

Stylish restaurant and bar that buzzes after work hours when young professionals drop by for a well-made cocktail and delicious nibbles.

### Alibi

Liberty Hotel, 215 Charles Street; tel: 617-224-4000; www.libertyhotel.com; daily; T-stop: Charles/MGH

Housed in a former jail, this lounge bar fittingly serves drinks in the clink's former drunk tank with blown-up mugshots of Frank Sinatra and Lindsay Lohan leering at patrons, and a cocktail menu listing drinks like 'Doing Thyme.'

### The Beehive

541 Tremont Street; tel: 617-423-0069; www.beehiveboston.com; daily; T-stop: Back Bay

Lounge bar and restaurant with inventive interior design, stylish crowd, velvet ropes, and a long line on weekends, when there's often live jazz.

### Bell in Hand

45 Union Street; tel: 617-227-2098; www.bellinhand.com; daily; T-stop: Haymarket

With a prime corner location, this self-proclaimed 'oldest tavern in America' (established in 1785) is a great people watching spot. They have their own beer and a full menu of traditional bar food.

### Crossroads Irish Pub

495 Beacon Street; tel: 617-262-7371; www.crossroadspubboston.com; T-stop: Hynes

An Irish pub favored by the tenants of the local frat houses. Laid-back atmosphere, large TV screens broadcasting sports games, and dartboards upstairs.

### Enormous Room

567 Massachusetts Avenue, Cambridge; tel: 617-491-5550; www.enormous.tv; daily; T-stop: Central

What this far-from-large room lacks in size it makes up for in street cred. An inconspicuous glass door leads to an appealing lounge packed with groovers.

### Felt

533 Washington Street; tel: 617-350-5555; www.feltboston.com; Tue–Sun; T-stop: Boylston

Local celebs, such as Ben Affleck and Matt Damon, drop by this happening spot, which combines bar, billiard hall, restaurant, and DJs on Fridays and Saturdays. They have a dress code.

## Goody Glover's

50 Salem Street; tel: 617-367-6444; www.goodyglovers.com; daily; T-stop: Haymarket

Neighborhood landmark named after Irish widow Goodwife Ann Glover, the last Bostonian hanged in 1688 for practicing witchcraft. Traditional Irish grub and laid-back vibe.

## Grendel's Den

89 Winthrop Street, Cambridge; tel: 617-491-1160; www.grendelsden.com; daily; T-stop: Harvard

Unpretentious student hangout that gained notoriety in 1982 when it won a historic court case enabling them to use their liquor license within 10 feet of a church.

## Jacob Wirth

31 Stuart Street; tel: 617-338-8586; www.jacobwirth.com; daily; T-stop: Boylston Street

Time-warp pub and restaurant in the Theater District, established in 1868, serving an impressive list of beers to accompany the wurst and sauerkraut.

## J.J. Foley's Cafe

117 East Berkeley Street; tel: 617-728-9101; jjfoleysbostonpubbar restaurant.com; daily; T-stop: Arlington

One of a few family-run old-school taverns surviving the South End gen-trification wave. In business since 1909, including a Prohibition-era stint as a suspiciously popular shoe store, Foley's is favored by off-duty cops, newspapermen, and nearby factory workers for cheap pints and simple grub.

## Les Zygomates Bistro Wine Bar

129 South Street; tel: 617-542-5108; www.winebar.com; Mon–Sat; T-stop: South Station

This atmospheric French bistro offers 40 wines by the glass. Tuesday nights feature wine-tastings with food for $30.

## Lucky's Lounge

355 Congress Street; tel: 617-357-5825; www.luckyslounge.com; daily; T-stop: South Station

Old Blue Eyes' spirit lives on at Lucky's, where cool pervades in a warehouse lounge with old photographs and outstanding Martinis that recall Rat Pack hip.

## Middlesex

315 Massachusetts Avenue, Cambridge: tel: 617-868-6739; www.middlesexlounge.com; daily; T-stop: Central

At around 10pm the low, sleek furniture is rolled to the edges of the room, and the space becomes a dance floor packed with a hip, cosmopolitan crowd. Go before 11pm to skip the legendary line.

## River Gods

125 River Street, Cambridge; tel: 617-576-1881; www.rivergods online.com; daily; T-stop: Central

**Opening hours**
Bars, pubs, and lounges typically open around 4 or 5pm. By law they all have to stop serving alcohol at 2am (1am Sunday to Wednesday in Cambridge).

Neighborhood pub with a quirky sense of style. Local artwork, furniture that looks as though it was randomly picked from several second-hand shops, and alternative rock all add to its charm.

## Sevens Ale House
77 Charles Street; tel: 617-523-9074; daily; T-stop: Charles/MGH
Refreshingly down to earth for ritzy Beacon Hill, this small rustic pub gets pretty rowdy on game nights. A game of darts can become a dangerous sport on packed weekend evenings.

### Live Music

## Berklee Performance Centre
136 Massachusetts Avenue; tel: 617-747-2261; www.berklee bpc.com; T-stop: Hynes; charge
Flagship performance space of the prestigious college of music with a highly regarded jazz program that attracts students from around the globe. Past alumni include Quincy Jones, Melissa Etheridge, Donald Fagen, and Branford Marsalis.

## Club Passim
47 Palmer Street; tel: 617-492-5300; www.clubpassim.org; T-stop: Harvard; charge
The US's oldest folk club, Passim hosts a variety of local and national artists, focusing on folk, world, and bluegrass.

## House of Blues
15 Lansdowne Street; tel: 888-693-2583; www.houseofblues.com/ venues/clubvenues/boston; daily; T-stop: Kenmore; charge

Mid-sized rock concert venue that's one of the choice venues for chart-topping acts from the US and abroad.

## The Middle East Club
472 Massachusetts Avenue, Cambridge; tel: 617-864-3278; www.mid eastclub.com; T-stop: Central; charge
A variety of acts play in this complex's various rooms, where the walls are adorned with local artists' work.

## Paradise Rock Club
967–969 Commonwealth Avenue; tel: 617-562-8800; www.thedise. com; daily 6pm–2am; T-stop Pleasant Street; charge
Boston's top venue for established and up-and-coming rock and alt pop music talents. For over 25 years it has hosted everyone from U2 to Bloc Party.

## Regattabar
Charles Hotel, 1 Bennett Street, Cambridge; tel: 617-661-5000; www.regatt abarjazz.com; T-stop: Harvard; charge
Fashionable bar featuring well-known jazz and R&B acts in a sophisticated interior. Bookings recommended.

## Toad
1912 Massachusetts Avenue, Cambridge; tel: 617-497-4950; www. toadcambridge.com; Mon–Wed 5pm–1am, Thur–Sat 5pm–2am, Sun 6pm–1am; T-stop: Porter Square
Bands perform live every night at this cozy neighborhood bar (room for just 62 customers) with no cover charge. Pearl Jam have done impromptu gigs here when they are in town.

## T.T. the Bear's Place

10 Brookline Street, Cambridge; tel: 617-492-0082; www.ttthebears.com; daily; T-stop: Central; charge

One of the best places in greater Boston to catch live music, in a relaxed, friendly atmosphere. Last-minute tickets can be bought at the door with cash only.

## Wally's Café

427 Massachusetts Avenue; tel: 617-424-1408; www.wallyscafe.com; daily; T-stop: Massachusetts Avenue

Hole-in-the-wall bar with jamming locals performing nightly. Named after founder Joseph L. Walcott, who opened the original bar across the street in 1947.

**Above from far left:** studenty Grendel's Den *(see p.121)*; folk music at Club Passim.

Gay Scene

## The Alley

Pl Alley, 275 Washington Street; tel: 617-263-1449; www.thealleybar.com; daily; T-stop: Park Street

Flying the flag for the Downtown gay community, this casual, friendly pub is the home of the annual Bearapalooza for the hirsute and their admirers.

## Club Café

209 Columbus Avenue; tel: 617-536-0966; www.clubcafe.com; daily; T-stop: Arlington

Popular and large complex, with a dance space and video lounge to the rear and quieter bar and restaurant at the front.

## Fritz

26 Chandler Street; tel: 617-482-4428; fritzboston.com; daily; T-stop: Back Bay

Gay sports bar beneath the Chandler Hotel that has big plasma TVs screening whatever game is current; the vibe is friendly and relaxed.

## Ramrod

1254 Boylston Street; tel: 617-226-2986; www.ramrod-boston.com; daily; T-stop: Kenmore; charge

Grungy hangout with pool hall and a leather bar upstairs. Its busiest night is Friday when it has an all-black dress code for Machine nightclub downstairs.

## Dance Clubs

## Mojitos

48 Winter Street; tel: 617-988-8123; www.mojitoslounge.com; Thur–Sat 9pm–2am; T-stop: Boylston; charge

Multi-level club for those who move to a Latin beat or want to learn (lessons kick off at 9.15pm on Fridays).

## Royale

279 Tremont Street; tel: 617-338-7699; royaleboston.com; Fri–Sat; T-stop: Boylston; charge

One of Boston's largest clubs, with seven bars, balconies, and a huge dance floor that also hosts live performances.

## Underbar

275 Tremont Street; tel: 617-292-0080; www.underbaronline.com; Fri–Sun; T-stop: Boylston; charge

Subterranean club hosting Latin house music on Friday, straight-up house on Saturday and, on Sunday, a 'hot mess' that's one of the top regular gay dance nights in the city.

**Clubbing rules**
For dance clubs you will typically pay an entrance fee of between $10 and $20, depending on the night and the DJ playing. Strict liquor-licencing laws means all clubs shut at 2am, with the sole exception of the members-only club Rise (306 Stuart Street; tel: 671-423-7473; www.riseclub.us). Many places also enforce a dress code prohibiting sportswear, sneakers, and baseball caps. Check websites or call for details before heading out.

# CREDITS

**Insight Step by Step Boston**
**Written and updated by:** Simon Richmond
**Commissioning Editor**: Sarah Sweeney
**Series Editor**: Carine Tracanelli
**Map Production:** APA Cartography Department
**Picture Manager:** Steven Lawrence
**Art Editor:** Richard Cooke
**Production:** Tynan Dean and Linton Donaldson

**Photography by**: Apa: Richard, Daniela, and Abraham Nowitz (also Marcus Brooke, Mark Read, and Carlotta Junger), except: istock photo 8TL, 12TM, 26TL, 44TM, 76–7T, 84TL, 89TR, 90TL, 92TL, 92–3T, 94–5T, 122-123, 119TR; Jon Arnold 68–9T; Mary Evans 21; Peter Newark's American Pictures 20; Rex Features 68TL; courtesy of the Museum of Fine Arts, Boston 65TR, 65BL.

**Cover**: main image: Atlantide Phototravel/Corbis; bottom left and right: Abraham Nowitz/APA.

**Printed by**: CTPS-China

## CONTACTING THE EDITORS

We would appreciate it if readers would alert us to errors or outdated information by writing to us at insight@apaguide.co.uk or APA Publications, PO Box 7910, London SE1 1WE, UK.

www.insightguides.com

# DISTRIBUTION

*Worldwide*

**APA Publications GmbH & Co. Verlag KG**

(Singapore branch)

7030 Ang Mo Kio Ave 5

08-65 Northstar @ AMK, Singapore 569880

E-mail: apasin@singnet.com.sg

*UK and Ireland*

**Dorling Kindersley Ltd**

(a Penguin Group company)

80 Strand, London, WC2R 0RL, UK

E-mail: customerservice@uk.dk.com

*United States*

**Ingram Publisher Services**

One Ingram Blvd, PO Box 3006

La Vergne, TN 37086-1986

E-mail: customer.service@ingrampublisher
services.com

*Australia*

**Universal Publishers**

PO Box 307

St. Leonards, NSW 1590

E-mail: sales@universalpublishers.com.au

# INDEX

## A

Acorn Street **52**
accommodations **108–13**
Adams, Samuel **20, 26, 30, 85**
airport **104**
Alcott, Louisa May **29, 52, 53, 86, 87**
American football **18**
Ames-Webster Mansion **57–8**
Arlington Street Church **56**
Arthur M. Sackler Museum **42**

## B

Back Bay **56–61**
Back Bay Fens **62–3, 64–7**
baseball **18, 62–3**
basketball **18**
Battle Green, Lexington **85**
Battle Road **85–6**
Beacon Hill **50–5**
Beacon Street **54–5, 57**
Beauport, the Sleeper-McCann House, Gloucester **83**
beer **15**
bicycle rental **107**
Big Dig **13, 32, 72**
Blackstone Block **31**
Blackstone Square **70**
Boston Athenaeum **51**
Boston Center for Adult Education **57**
Boston Center for the Arts **71**
Boston Children's Museum **75**
Boston City Hall **30**
Boston Common **24, 25–6**
Boston Marathon **19**
Boston Massacre monument **30**
Boston Pops Esplanade Orchestra **19, 49**
Boston Public Library **59**
Boston Stone **31**
Boston Tea Party **29, 72**
Boston Tea Party Ships and Museum **74–5**

Braddock Park **68–9**
Bulfinch, Charles **12, 34, 40, 51, 52, 55**
Bumpkin Island **77**
Bunker Hill Monument and Museum **38–9**
Burrage House **58**
Busch-Reisinger Museum **42, 43**
buses **105, 106**

## C

Cambridge **40–5, 48–9**
Cambridge Common **44**
CambridgeSide Galleria **48**
Cape Ann **82–3**
Cape Cod National Seashore **94**
Carleton Court Park **68**
Carpenter Center for the Visual Arts **42**
car rental **107**
Cathedral of the Holy Cross **70**
Center for Latino Arts **69**
Central Burying Ground **25–6**
Charles Hayden Planetarium **47**
Charles River **10, 45, 46–9**
Charles Street **17, 54**
Charles Street Meeting House **54**
Charlestown **37–9**
Charlestown Bridge **37**
Charlestown Navy Yard **37**
Chester Square **70**
Chestnut Street **52**
Chinatown **24**
Christian Science Church **61**
Christian Science Plaza **61**
City Hall Plaza **30**
City Square **37**
climate **98**
Columbus Park **73**
Commonwealth Avenue **56–8**
Community Boating **49**
Concord **86–7**
consulates **98**

Copley Place **16, 60**
Copley Square **59–60**
Copp's Hill Burying Ground **36**
crime and safety **99**
Curley, James **31**
Custom House **74**
customs **99**

## D

DeCordova Museum and Sculpture Park **87**
disabled travellers **99**
Downtown **24–31**
driving **105, 107**
Duck Tours **60**
Dyer, Mary **25, 51**

## E

Emerald Necklace **10, 63**
Emerson, Ralph Waldo **29, 51, 86, 87**
entertainment **18–19**
Esplanade **49**

## F

Faneuil Hall **30, 72–3**
Fenway Park **62–3**
Fenway Victory Gardens **63**
Filene's Basement **17**
First Baptist Church **57**
Fogg Art Museum **42, 43**
food and drink **14–15, 114–19**
Fort Point **74–5**
Franklin, Benjamin **28, 29**
Franklin Square **70**
Freedom Trail **25–31, 32–9**
Frog Pond **26**

## G

Gardner, Isabella Stewart **57, 66–7**
Garrison, William Lloyd **26, 53**

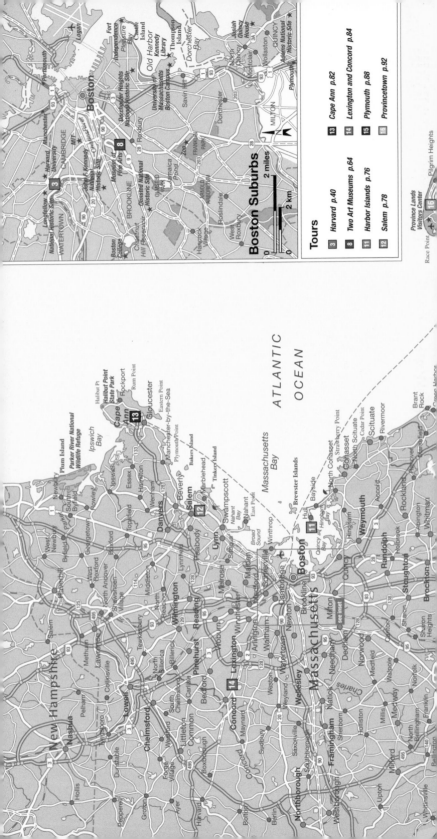

## Boston Suburbs

### Tours

3  *Harvard p.40*
8  *Two Art Museums p.64*
11 *Harbor Islands p.76*
12 *Salem p.78*
13 *Cape Ann p.82*
14 *Lexington and Concord p.84*
15 *Plymouth p.88*
16 *Provincetown p.92*

0    2 miles

0    2 km